everyday
chinese

This edition published in 2010
LOVE FOOD is an imprint of Parragon Books Ltd

Parragon
Queen Street House
4 Queen Street
Bath BA1 1HE, UK

ISBN: 978-1-4075-2797-0

Printed In China

Designed by Terry Jeavons & Company

Notes for the Reader
This book uses both metric and imperial measurements. Follow the same units of measurement throughout; do not mix metric and imperial. All spoon measurements are level: teaspoons are assumed to be 5 ml, and tablespoons are assumed to be 15 ml. Unless otherwise stated, milk is assumed to be full fat, eggs and individual vegetables are medium, and pepper is freshly ground black pepper.

The times given are an approximate guide only. Preparation times differ according to the techniques used by different people and the cooking times may also vary from those given. Optional ingredients, variations or serving suggestions have not been included in the calculations.

Recipes using raw or very lightly cooked eggs should be avoided by infants, the elderly, pregnant women, convalescents and anyone suffering from an illness. Pregnant and breastfeeding women are advised to avoid eating peanuts and peanut products. Sufferers from nut allergies should be aware that some of the ready-made ingredients used in the recipes in this book may contain nuts. Always check the packaging before use.

everyday
chinese

introduction

Most people enjoy good Chinese food, and this is perhaps because the Chinese people's respect for their cuisine is reflected in the food itself. Cooking is considered to be an art, not a necessary chore, and indeed Chinese dishes are every bit as beautiful to look at as they are delicious to eat.

A vast population inhabiting an often rugged, agriculturally barren landscape has led to creative use of the available ingredients. Many crops, including potatoes, tomatoes and aubergines, were introduced by foreigners and have been absorbed into the Chinese culinary culture mainly because they grow successfully in poor soil.

Traditionally in China, and still today, there is a vitally important relationship between food and health. This manifests in two distinct ways. Firstly, there is a closely observed balance between carbohydrate foods, mostly in the form of rice or grains, and all other foods, from meat, fish and seafood to fresh and preserved vegetables. Secondly, foods are further divided into two groups, *yin* and *yang*. Yang are 'heating' foods, such as beef,  carrots and chillies, associated with masculinity, while yin are 'cooling' foods – crab, watercress and cucumber – associated with femininity. Thus, the composition of a meal takes account not only of what is in season or looks good at the market, but also of the age, gender and state of health of the diners, and the weather!

If all you want, however, is an appetizing meal that is quick and easy to cook and has marvellous colour, flavour and texture, simply choose your favourite recipes and enjoy yourself! To eat Chinese-

style, especially when you have guests, serve several dishes and have a little of everything – remember to aim for balance. Pretty Chinese serving bowls will enhance the menu, and of course chopsticks add to the fun.

A toast to your very good health!

soups &
starters

Soups are one of the mainstays of the Chinese diet. They are almost exclusively light, clear broths with the addition of a little meat, seafood or tofu, and sometimes noodles, together with seasonal vegetables and fresh herbs. They are not served, Western-style, at the start of a meal, but are eaten throughout the meal, or even at the end – delicate Szechuan Pumpkin Soup, for example, freshens the palate after a series of spicy dishes. Soups are also eaten for breakfast, or as a snack throughout the day, and are certainly nutritious and satisfying enough to make a perfect light lunch or supper dish. Wonton Soup is definitely a meal in itself – use good quality chicken stock as the base and be generous with the wontons.

The Chinese do not necessarily serve separate Western-style 'starters' either, but have a vast array of snack foods in their culinary repertoire, to be found on food stalls everywhere – the things we all know and love, such as Spring Rolls, Prawn Toasts, Soy Chicken Wings and Crispy Crab Wontons. These make excellent starters in a marriage of Western and Eastern cuisines, and you can add a few dishes that you might not have tried – soft, melting Onion Pancakes, Tea-scented Eggs and Lettuce Wraps, which your guests can assemble themselves.

wonton soup

ingredients

SERVES 6

30 square wonton skins

1 egg white, lightly beaten

2 tbsp finely chopped spring
onion, to serve

1 tbsp chopped coriander
leaves, to garnish

filling

175 g/6 oz pork mince,
not too lean

225 g/8 oz raw prawns,
peeled, deveined and
chopped

^{1}/$_2$ tsp finely chopped
fresh ginger

1 tbsp light soy sauce

1 tbsp Shaoxing rice wine

2 tsp finely chopped spring
onion

pinch of sugar

pinch of white pepper

dash of sesame oil

soup

2 litres/3^1/$_2$ pints chicken
stock

2 tsp salt

^{1}/$_2$ tsp white pepper

method

1 Mix together the filling ingredients and stir
well until the texture is thick and pasty. Set
aside for at least 20 minutes.

2 To make the wontons, place a teaspoon
of the filling in the centre of a skin. Brush
the edges with a little egg white. Bring the
opposite points towards each other and press
the edges together, creating a flower-like
shape. Repeat with the remaining skins
and filling.

3 To make the soup, bring the stock to the
boil in a large saucepan and add the salt
and pepper. Boil the wontons in the stock
for about 5 minutes, or until the skins begin
to wrinkle around the filling.

4 To serve, put the spring onion in individual
bowls, then spoon in the wontons and soup
and top with the coriander.

crab & sweetcorn soup

ingredients

SERVES 4

115 g/4 oz fresh or frozen
    crabmeat

600 ml/1 pint water

425 g/15 oz canned
    creamed sweetcorn,
    drained

1/2 tsp salt

pinch of pepper

2 tsp cornflour, dissolved in
    2 tbsp water (optional)

1 egg, beaten

method

1 If using frozen crabmeat, blanch the flesh
in boiling water for 30 seconds. Remove with
a slotted spoon and set aside.

2 In a large saucepan, bring the water to the
boil with the crab and sweetcorn and simmer
for 2 minutes. Season with the salt and pepper.
Stir in the cornflour, if using, and continue
stirring until the soup has thickened. Rapidly
stir in the egg and serve.

beef mince
& coriander soup

ingredients

SERVES 4–6

225 g/8 oz beef mince

1.7 litres/3 pints chicken
   stock

3 egg whites, lightly beaten

1 tsp salt

1/2 tsp white pepper

1 tbsp finely chopped
   fresh ginger

1 tbsp finely chopped
   spring onion

4–5 tbsp finely chopped
   coriander, tough stems
   discarded

marinade

1 tsp salt

1 tsp sugar

1 tsp Shaoxing rice wine

1 tsp light soy sauce

method

1 Combine all the ingredients for the marinade in a bowl and add the beef. Allow to marinate for 20 minutes.

2 Bring the stock to the boil in a large saucepan. Add the beef, stirring to break up any clumps, and simmer for 10 minutes.

3 Slowly add the egg whites, stirring rapidly so that they form into fine shreds. Add the salt and pepper and taste to check the seasoning.

4 To serve, place the ginger, spring onion and coriander in the base of each individual bowl and pour the soup on top.

tofu & beansprout soup

ingredients

SERVES 4–6

280 g/10 oz spare ribs, cut
    into small pieces
1.2 litres/2 pints water
2 tomatoes, deseeded and
    roughly chopped
3 thin slices fresh ginger
140 g/5 oz beansprouts
2 tsp salt
200 g/7 oz soft tofu, cut into
    2.5-cm/1-inch cubes

method

1 Bring a saucepan of water to the boil and blanch the spare ribs for about 30 seconds. Skim the water, then remove the ribs and set aside.

2 Bring the measured water to the boil in a large saucepan and add the spare ribs, tomatoes and ginger. After 10 minutes, remove the tomato skins from the water. Add the beansprouts and salt, then cover and simmer for 1 hour. Add the tofu cubes and simmer for a further 2 minutes, then serve.

hot-&-sour soup

ingredients

SERVES 4–5

3 dried Chinese mushrooms,
    soaked in warm water for
    20 minutes

115 g/4 oz pork loin

55 g/2 oz fresh or canned
    bamboo shoots, rinsed (if
    using fresh shoots, boil in
    water first for 30 minutes)

225 g/8 oz firm tofu

850 ml/1$^1/_2$ pints chicken
    stock

1 tbsp Shaoxing rice wine

1 tbsp light soy sauce

1$^1/_2$ tbsp white rice vinegar

1 tsp salt

1 tsp white pepper

1 egg, lightly beaten

method

1 Squeeze out any excess water from the
mushrooms, then finely slice, discarding any
tough stems. Finely slice the pork, bamboo
shoots and tofu, all to a similar size.

2 Bring the stock to the boil in a large saucepan.
Add the pork and boil over a high heat for
2 minutes. Add the mushrooms and bamboo
shoots and boil for a further 2 minutes. Next,
add the Shaoxing, light soy sauce, rice vinegar,
salt and pepper. Bring back to the boil and
simmer, covered, for 5 minutes. Add the tofu
and boil, uncovered, for 2 minutes.

3 To serve, rapidly stir in the egg until it has
formed fine shreds. Serve immediately.

whole chicken soup

ingredients

SERVES 6–8

100 g/3^1/$_2$ oz Yunnan ham or
   ordinary ham, chopped

2 dried Chinese mushrooms,
   soaked in warm water for
   20 minutes

85 g/3 oz fresh or canned
   bamboo shoots, rinsed (if
   using fresh shoots, boil in
   water first for 30 minutes)

1 whole chicken

1 tbsp slivered spring onion

8 slices fresh ginger

225 g/8 oz lean pork,
   chopped

2 tsp Shaoxing rice wine

3 litres/5^1/$_4$ pints water

2 tsp salt

300 g/10^1/$_2$ oz Chinese
   cabbage, cut into large
   chunks

sesame & spring onion dipping sauce

2 tbsp light soy sauce

^{1}/$_4$ tsp sesame oil

2 tsp finely chopped
   spring onion

method

1 To make the dipping sauce, combine the ingredients and set aside.

2 Blanch the Yunnan ham in a large saucepan of boiling water for 30 seconds. Skim the surface, then remove the ham and set aside. Squeeze out any excess water from the mushrooms, then finely slice and discard any tough stems. Chop the bamboo shoots into small cubes.

3 Stuff the chicken with the spring onion and ginger. Put all the ingredients except the cabbage and dipping sauce in a casserole. Bring to the boil, then lower the heat and simmer, covered, for 1 hour. Add the cabbage and simmer for a further 3 minutes.

4 Remove the chicken skin before serving, then place a chunk of chicken meat in individual bowls, adding pieces of vegetable and the other meats, and pour the soup on top. Serve with the dipping sauce.

chinese mushroom soup

ingredients

SERVES 4

115 g/4 oz dried thin Chinese
    egg noodles
15 g/^{1}/$_2$ oz dried Chinese
    wood ear mushrooms,
    soaked in boiling water for
    20 minutes
2 tsp arrowroot or cornflour
1 litre/1^3/$_4$ pints vegetable
    stock
5-cm/2-inch piece fresh
    ginger, peeled and sliced
2 tbsp dark soy sauce
2 tsp mirin or sweet sherry
1 tsp rice vinegar
4 small pak choi, each cut
    in half
salt and pepper
snipped fresh Chinese or
    ordinary chives, to garnish

method

1 Boil the noodles for 3 minutes or according to the packet instructions, until soft. Drain well, rinse with cold water to stop the cooking, and set aside.

2 Strain the mushrooms through a sieve lined with a tea towel and reserve the liquid. Leave the mushrooms whole or slice them, depending on how large they are. Put the arrowroot in a wok or large saucepan and gradually stir in the reserved mushroom liquid. Add the vegetable stock, sliced ginger, soy sauce, mirin, rice vinegar, mushrooms and pak choi and bring the mixture to the boil, stirring constantly. Lower the heat and simmer for 15 minutes.

3 Add salt and pepper, but remember that soy sauce is salty so you might not need any salt at all – taste first. Use a slotted spoon to remove the pieces of ginger.

4 Divide the noodles between 4 bowls, then spoon the soup over and garnish with chives.

chinese vegetable soup

ingredients

SERVES 4–6

115 g/4 oz Napa cabbage

2 tbsp peanut oil

225 g/8 oz firm marinated
    tofu, cut into 1-cm/
    $^1/_2$-inch cubes

2 garlic cloves, thinly sliced

4 spring onions, thinly sliced
    diagonally

1 carrot, thinly sliced

1 litre/1$^3/_4$ pints vegetable
    stock

1 tbsp Chinese rice wine

2 tbsp light soy sauce

1 tsp sugar

salt and pepper

method

1 Shred the Napa cabbage and set aside.
Heat the oil in a large preheated wok or frying
pan over a high heat. Add the tofu cubes and
stir-fry for 4–5 minutes until browned. Remove
from the wok with a slotted spoon and drain
on kitchen paper.

2 Add the garlic, spring onions and carrot to
the wok and stir-fry for 2 minutes. Pour in the
stock, rice wine and soy sauce, then add the
sugar and shredded Napa cabbage. Cook over
a medium heat, stirring, for a further 1–2
minutes until heated through.

3 Season with salt and pepper and return the
tofu to the wok. Ladle the soup into warmed
bowls and serve.

szechuan pumpkin soup

ingredients

SERVES 4–6

1 litre/1³/4 pints chicken stock

450 g/1 lb pumpkin, peeled
and cut into small cubes

1 tbsp chopped preserved
vegetables

1 tsp white pepper

115 g/4 oz any leafy green
Chinese vegetable,
shredded

salt (optional)

method

1 Bring the stock to the boil in a large saucepan, then stir in the pumpkin and simmer for 4–5 minutes.

2 Add the preserved vegetables with the pepper and stir. Finally, add the green vegetable. Season with salt, if liked. Simmer for a further minute and serve.

soft-wrapped pork & prawn rolls

ingredients

MAKES 20

115 g/4 oz firm tofu

3 tbsp vegetable or peanut oil

1 tsp finely chopped garlic

55 g/2 oz lean pork, shredded

115 g/4 oz raw prawns,
   peeled and deveined

1/2 small carrot, cut into short
   thin sticks

55 g/2 oz fresh or canned
   bamboo shoots, rinsed
   and shredded (if using
   fresh shoots, boil in water
   first for 30 minutes)

115 g/4 oz very finely sliced
   cabbage

55 g/2 oz mangetout,
   julienned

1-egg omelette, shredded

1 tsp salt

1 tsp light soy sauce

1 tsp Shaoxing rice wine

pinch of white pepper

20 soft spring roll skins

chilli bean sauce, to serve

method

1 Slice the tofu into thin slices horizontally and cook in 1 tablespoon of the oil until it turns golden brown. Cut into thin strips and set aside.

2 In a preheated wok or deep saucepan, heat the remaining oil and stir-fry the garlic until fragrant. Add the pork and stir for about 1 minute, then add the prawns and stir for a further minute. One by one, stirring well after each addition, add the carrot, bamboo shoots, cabbage, mangetout, tofu and, finally, the shredded omelette. Season with the salt, light soy sauce, Shaoxing rice wine and pepper. Stir for one more minute, then turn into a serving dish.

3 To assemble each roll, smear a skin with a little chilli bean sauce and place a heaped teaspoon of the filling towards the bottom of the circle. Roll up the bottom edge to secure the filling, turn in the sides, and continue to roll up gently. Serve accompanied by a bowl of chilli sauce.

pork & ginger dumplings

ingredients

MAKES ABOUT 50

450 g/1 lb pork mince, not
    too lean
1 tbsp light soy sauce
1 1/2 tsp salt
1 tsp Shaoxing rice wine
1/2 tsp sesame oil
100 g/3 1/2 oz very finely
    chopped cabbage
2 tsp minced fresh ginger
2 tsp finely chopped
    spring onions
1/2 tsp white pepper
50 round wonton skins,
    about 7 cm/2 3/4 inches
    in diameter

ginger & garlic dipping sauce

1 tbsp soy sauce
1 tbsp vinegar
1/2 tsp sugar
1 tsp chopped fresh ginger
1 tsp chopped garlic

method

1 To make the dipping sauce, stir all the ingredients together and set aside.

2 For the filling, mix the pork with the light soy sauce and 1/2 teaspoon salt. Stir carefully, always in the same direction, to create a thick paste. Add the Shaoxing and sesame oil and continue mixing in the same direction. Cover and let rest for at least 20 minutes.

3 Meanwhile, sprinkle the cabbage with the remaining salt to help draw out the water. Add the ginger, spring onions and white pepper and knead for at least 5 minutes into a thick paste. Combine with the filling.

4 To make the dumplings, place about 1 tablespoon of the filling in the centre of each skin, holding the skin in the palm of one hand. Moisten the edges with water, then seal the edges with 2 or 3 pleats on each side and place on a lightly floured board.

5 To cook the dumplings, bring 1 litre/1 3/4 pints of water to a rolling boil in a large saucepan. Drop in about 20 dumplings at a time, stirring gently with a chopstick to prevent them sticking together. Cover, then bring back to the boil and cook for 2 minutes. Uncover and add about 225 ml/7 fl oz of cold water. Bring back to the boil, cover and cook for a further 2 minutes. Serve the dumplings with individual bowls of dipping sauce.

spring rolls

ingredients

MAKES 25

6 dried Chinese mushrooms,
    soaked in warm water for
    20 minutes
1 tbsp vegetable or peanut oil
225 g/8 oz pork mince
1 tsp dark soy sauce
100 g/3$^1/_2$ oz fresh or canned
    bamboo shoots, rinsed
    and julienned (if using
    fresh shoots, boil in water
    first for 30 minutes)
pinch of salt
100 g/3$^1/_2$ oz raw prawns,
    peeled, deveined and
    chopped
225 g/8 oz beansprouts,
    trimmed and roughly
    chopped
1 tbsp finely chopped
    spring onions
25 spring roll skins
1 egg white, lightly beaten
vegetable or peanut oil, for
    deep-frying

method

1 Squeeze out any excess water from the
mushrooms and finely slice, discarding any
tough stems.

2 In a preheated wok or deep saucepan, heat
the tablespoon of oil and stir-fry the pork until
it changes colour. Add the dark soy sauce,
bamboo shoots, mushrooms and a little salt.
Stir over a high heat for 3 minutes.

3 Add the prawns and cook for 2 minutes,
then add the beansprouts and cook for a
further minute. Remove from the heat, stir
in the spring onions and set aside to cool.

4 Place a tablespoon of the mixture towards
the bottom of a skin. Roll once to secure
the filling, then fold in the sides to create a
10-cm/4-inch piece and continue to roll up.
Seal with egg white.

5 Heat enough oil for deep-frying in a wok,
deep-fat fryer or large heavy-based saucepan
to 180–190°C/350–375°F, or until a cube
of bread browns in 30 seconds. Without
overcrowding the pan, fry the rolls for about
5 minutes until golden brown and crispy. Drain
well on kitchen paper and serve immediately.

dumplings in a cold spicy sauce

ingredients

MAKES 20

20 square wheat skins

filling

1 tsp vegetable or peanut oil

200 g/7 oz pork mince, not too lean

1 tsp salt

$1/2$ tsp white pepper

sauce

100 ml/$3^1/_2$ fl oz vegetable or peanut oil

1 tbsp dried chilli flakes

1 tsp sesame oil

1 tsp sugar

1 tbsp light soy sauce

$1/2$ tsp white pepper

1 tsp salt

1 garlic clove, finely chopped

method

1 To prepare the filling, heat the oil in a small saucepan and stir-fry the pork with the salt and pepper for 3–4 minutes, stirring to break up any meat clumps and letting the juices begin to come out.

2 To prepare the sauce, heat the oil until smoking in a wok or deep saucepan and pour over the chilli flakes. Allow to cool, then stir in all the other ingredients.

3 To make the dumplings, hold a skin in the palm of one hand and place a scant teaspoon of the filling in the centre. Wet the edges and fold over to create a triangle, then, with the point facing towards you at the bottom of your index finger, cross the edges behind your finger, sealing with a little water. Take the point facing towards you and turn up to form a wonton.

4 Drop the dumplings into a large saucepan of boiling water and cook for 5 minutes.

5 To serve, assemble 4 or 5 pieces per serving on a small plate and pour over a generous amount of the sauce.

soy chicken wings

ingredients

SERVES 3–4

250 g/9 oz chicken wings,
   defrosted if frozen

250 ml/9 fl oz water

1 tbsp sliced spring onion

2.5-cm/1-inch piece of fresh
   ginger, cut into 4 slices

2 tbsp light soy sauce

$1/2$ tsp dark soy sauce

1 star anise

1 tsp sugar

method

1 Wash and dry the chicken wings. In a small saucepan, bring the water to the boil, then add the chicken, spring onion and ginger and bring back to the boil.

2 Add the remaining ingredients, then cover and simmer for 30 minutes.

3 Remove the chicken wings from any remaining liquid and serve hot.

whitebait with green chilli

ingredients

SERVES 4

175 g/6 oz whitebait

sauce

1 tbsp vegetable or peanut oil

1 large fresh green chilli

2 drops of sesame oil

1 tbsp light soy sauce

pinch of salt

pinch of sugar

1 garlic clove, finely chopped

method

1 In a large saucepan of boiling water, cook the fish for 30 seconds–2 minutes, or until the flesh is turning soft but not breaking up. Drain, then set aside to cool.

2 To prepare the sauce, first heat the oil in a small saucepan and, when smoking, cook the chilli until the skin blisters. Remove the skin and finely chop the chilli. When cool, mix with all the other ingredients.

3 To serve, pour the sauce over the fish and serve immediately.

prawn toasts

ingredients

MAKES 16

100 g/3¹/₂ oz raw prawns,
    peeled and deveined
2 egg whites
2 tbsp cornflour
¹/₂ tsp sugar
pinch of salt
2 tbsp finely chopped
    coriander leaves
2 slices day-old white bread
vegetable or peanut oil, for
    deep-frying

method

1 Pound the prawns to a pulp in a mortar and pestle or with the base of a cleaver.

2 Mix the prawns with one of the egg whites and 1 tablespoon of the cornflour. Add the sugar and salt and stir in the coriander. Mix the remaining egg white with the remaining cornflour.

3 Remove the crusts from the bread and cut each slice into 8 triangles. Brush the top of each piece with the egg white and cornflour mixture, then add 1 teaspoon of the prawn mixture. Smooth the top.

4 Heat enough oil for deep-frying in a wok, deep-fat fryer or large heavy-based saucepan to 180–190°C/350–375°F, or until a cube of bread browns in 30 seconds. Without overcrowding the wok, cook the toasts prawn-side up for about 2 minutes. Turn and cook for a further 2 minutes, or until beginning to turn golden brown. Drain and serve warm.

crispy crab wontons

ingredients

MAKES 24

175 g/6 oz white crabmeat,
    drained if canned and
    thawed if frozen, flaked
50 g/1³/4 oz canned water
    chestnuts, drained, rinsed
    and chopped
1 small fresh red chilli,
    chopped
1 spring onion, chopped
1 tbsp cornflour
1 tsp dry sherry
1 tsp light soy sauce
¹/2 tsp lime juice
24 wonton skins
vegetable oil, for deep-frying
lime slices, to garnish

method

1 To make the filling, mix the crabmeat, water chestnuts, chilli, spring onion, cornflour, sherry, soy sauce and lime juice together in a bowl.

2 Spread the wonton skins out on a work surface and spoon an equal portion of the filling into the centre of each wonton skin.

3 Dampen the edges of the wonton skins with a little water and fold them in half to form triangles. Fold the 2 pointed ends in towards the centre, moisten with a little water to secure, then pinch together to seal.

4 Heat the oil in a wok, deep-fat fryer or large, heavy-based saucepan to 180–190°C/350–375°F, or until a cube of bread browns in 30 seconds. Deep-fry the wontons in batches for 2–3 minutes until golden brown and crisp (if you deep-fry too many at one time, the oil temperature will drop and they will be soggy).

5 Remove the wontons with a slotted spoon, drain on kitchen paper and serve hot, garnished with lime slices.

pickled baby cucumbers

ingredients

SERVES 4

1 tbsp vegetable or peanut
    oil, for frying

400 g/14 oz baby cucumbers

500 ml/18 fl oz white
    rice vinegar

1 tbsp salt

3 tbsp sugar

3 red Thai chillies, deseeded
    and finely chopped

method

1 In a wok or deep saucepan, heat the oil and cook the cucumbers for 3–5 minutes, or until they are bright green. Drain and set aside. When cool, score the skin many times on all sides. Place in a large dish.

2 Combine the vinegar, salt, sugar and chilli and pour over the cucumbers, immersing them in the liquid. Marinate for 24 hours, then serve cold in chunks.

lettuce wraps

ingredients

MAKES 12

100 g/3¹/₂ oz dried
    cellophane noodles

3 tbsp crunchy peanut butter

2 tbsp rice vinegar

1 tbsp oyster sauce

peanut or corn oil (optional)

soy sauce, to taste

4 red radishes, grated

2 carrots, peeled and
    roughly grated

1 courgette, roughly grated

115 g/4 oz canned sweetcorn
    kernels, drained

12 large lettuce leaves,
    such as iceberg, rinsed
    and dried

dipping sauce

10 tbsp rice vinegar

4 tbsp clear honey

2 tbsp toasted sesame oil

1 tsp bottled chilli sauce

2.5-cm/1-inch piece fresh
    ginger, peeled and very
    finely chopped

method

1 Put the noodles in a bowl, pour over enough lukewarm water to cover and soak for 20 minutes, until soft. Alternatively, follow the packet instructions. Drain and rinse, then cut into 7.5-cm/3-inch lengths.

2 Beat the peanut butter, vinegar and oyster sauce together in a large bowl, adding a little oil to lighten the mixture, if necessary. Toss with the noodles in the bowl to coat, then add soy sauce to taste. Cover and chill until 15 minutes before you plan to serve.

3 Meanwhile, mix together the dipping sauce ingredients in a small bowl.

4 When you are ready to serve, stir the radishes, carrots, courgette and sweetcorn into the noodles and transfer to a serving dish. To assemble the lettuce wraps, place some noodles in a lettuce leaf and roll up the leaf to enclose the filling.

onion pancakes

ingredients

MAKES ABOUT 16

4 tbsp oil

4 tbsp finely sliced
    spring onions

2 eggs, plus 2 egg yolks

200 g/7 oz plain flour

1 tsp salt

400 ml/14 fl oz milk

225 ml/8 fl oz water

method

1 Heat 1 tablespoon of the oil in a frying pan
and lightly cook the spring onions until
beginning to soften. Remove and set aside.

2 Lightly beat the eggs, together with the egg
yolks, and set aside. Sift the flour and salt into
a large bowl and lightly mix in the eggs.

3 Slowly add the milk and water, beating by
hand, until the batter is creamy. Stir in the
remaining oil and continue to beat for a few
more minutes. Finally, stir in the spring onions.

4 Heat a non-stick frying pan, pour in
1 tablespoon of the batter and cook until set,
but not brown. To serve, loosely roll the
pancakes and cut each one into 3 pieces.

vegetarian spring rolls

ingredients

MAKES 20

6 dried Chinese mushrooms,
    soaked in warm water for
    20 minutes

55 g/2 oz beanthread
    noodles, soaked in warm
    water for 20 minutes

2 tbsp vegetable or peanut oil

1 tbsp finely chopped
    fresh ginger

100 g/3^1/$_2$ oz carrot, julienned

100 g/3^1/$_2$ oz finely shredded
    cabbage

1 tbsp finely sliced
    spring onions

1 tbsp light soy sauce

85 g/3 oz soft tofu,
    cut into small cubes

^{1}/$_2$ tsp salt

pinch of white pepper

pinch of sugar

20 spring roll skins

1 egg white, lightly beaten

vegetable or peanut oil,
    for deep-frying

soy sauce, for dipping

method

1 Squeeze out any excess water from the mushrooms and finely chop, discarding any tough stems. Drain the beanthread noodles and roughly chop.

2 In a preheated wok or deep saucepan, heat the oil, then toss in the ginger and cook until fragrant. Add the mushrooms and stir for about 2 minutes. Add the carrot, cabbage and spring onions and stir-fry for 1 minute. Add the beanthread noodles and light soy sauce and stir-fry for 1 minute. Add the tofu and cook for a further 1 minute. Season with the salt, pepper and sugar and mix well. Continue cooking for 1–2 minutes, or until the carrot is soft. Remove from the heat and allow to cool.

3 Place a scant tablespoon of the mixture towards the bottom of a skin. Roll once to secure the filling, then fold in the sides to create a 10-cm/4-inch width and continue to roll up. Seal with egg white.

4 Heat enough oil for deep-frying in a wok, deep-fat fryer or large, heavy-based saucepan to 180–190°C/350–375°F, or until a cube of bread browns in 30 seconds. Without overcrowding the pan, cook the rolls in batches for about 5 minutes, or until golden brown and crispy. Serve with a good soy sauce for dipping.

tea-scented eggs

ingredients

SERVES 6

6 eggs

water, about 100 ml/18 fl oz

2 tbsp black tea leaves

method

1 Bring to the boil a saucepan of water deep enough to cover the eggs. Lower the eggs into the saucepan and cook for 10 minutes. Remove the eggs from the saucepan and lightly crack the shells with the back of a spoon.

2 Bring the water back to the boil, add the tea leaves and simmer for 5 minutes. Turn off the heat. Place the eggs in the tea and let stand until the tea has cooled.

3 Serve the eggs whole for breakfast or as part of a meal, shelled or, more traditionally, unshelled.

main dishes

One of the great joys of Chinese cooking is that it takes very little time to produce a really attractive, filling main dish. We tend, for example, to expect a casserole to need long, slow cooking, but the Xinjiang Lamb Casserole is ready to serve in less than 45 minutes – and this is the dish in this chapter with the longest cooking time! Even those recipes that require a little time for preparing the ingredients or marinating the meat or fish take only a few minutes to cook.

The main reason behind the welcome speed of Chinese dishes is the use of the wok, the most important item of equipment in an Asian kitchen. The curved shape enables the heat to be distributed quickly and evenly, and food is stir-fried for only as long as it takes to cook. Vegetables retain their vibrant colour and nutritional value, while meat, which is usually cut into small pieces, is rapidly sealed and retains its juices, making it succulent and delicious. Flavourings such as ginger and chilli add excitement, and sauces cloak the ingredients and ooze into the rice or noodles that invariably accompany the meal.

Fish also gets the stir-fry treatment, or is steamed or deep-fried – Steamed Sole with Black Bean Sauce can be cooked in a foil package and emerges tasting just wonderful!

marinated beef with vegetables

ingredients

SERVES 4

500 g/1 lb 2 oz rump steak, cut into thin strips

3 tbsp sesame oil

1/2 tbsp cornflour

1/2 tbsp soy sauce

1 head of broccoli, cut into florets

2 carrots, cut into thin strips

125 g/4 oz mangetout

125 ml/4 fl oz beef stock

250 g/9 oz baby spinach, shredded

freshly cooked rice or noodles, to serve

marinade

1 tbsp dry sherry

1/2 tbsp soy sauce

1/2 tbsp cornflour

1/2 tsp caster sugar

2 garlic cloves, chopped finely

1 tbsp sesame oil

method

1 To make the marinade, mix the sherry, soy sauce, cornflour, sugar, garlic and sesame oil in a bowl. Add the beef to the mixture and cover with clingfilm. Set aside to marinate for 30 minutes, then remove the beef and discard the marinade.

2 Heat 1 tablespoon of the sesame oil in a frying pan or wok. Stir-fry the beef for 2 minutes until medium-rare. Remove from the frying pan and set aside.

3 Combine the cornflour and soy sauce in a bowl and set aside. Pour the remaining 2 tablespoons of sesame oil into the frying pan, add the broccoli, carrots and mangetout and stir-fry for 2 minutes.

4 Add the stock, cover the frying pan and steam for one minute. Stir in the spinach, beef and the cornflour mixture. Cook until the juices boil and thicken. Serve on a bed of freshly cooked rice or noodles.

beef chop suey

ingredients

SERVES 4

450 g/1 lb ribeye or sirloin
    steak, finely sliced

1 head of broccoli, cut into
    small florets

2 tbsp vegetable or peanut oil

1 onion, finely sliced

2 celery sticks, finely sliced
    diagonally

225 g/8 oz mangetout, sliced
    in half lengthways

55 g/2 oz fresh or canned
    bamboo shoots, rinsed
    and julienned (if using
    fresh shoots, boil in water
    first for 30 minutes)

8 water chestnuts, finely sliced

225 g/8 oz finely sliced
    mushrooms

1 tbsp oyster sauce

1 tsp salt

marinade

1 tbsp Shaoxing rice wine

pinch of white pepper

pinch of salt

1 tbsp light soy sauce

$1/2$ tsp sesame oil

method

1 Combine all the marinade ingredients in a bowl and marinate the beef for at least 20 minutes. Blanch the broccoli florets in a large saucepan of boiling water for 30 seconds. Drain and set aside.

2 In a preheated wok or deep saucepan, heat 1 tablespoon of the oil and stir-fry the beef until the colour has changed. Remove and set aside.

3 In the clean wok or deep saucepan, heat the remaining oil and stir-fry the onion for 1 minute. Add the celery and broccoli and cook for 2 minutes. Add the mangetout, bamboo shoots, chestnuts and mushrooms and cook for 1 minute. Add the beef, then season with the oyster sauce and salt and serve immediately.

hot sesame beef

ingredients

SERVES 4

500 g/1 lb 2 oz beef fillet, cut
   into thin strips

1¹/₂ tbsp sesame seeds

125 ml/4 fl oz beef stock

2 tbsp soy sauce

2 tbsp grated fresh ginger

2 garlic cloves, finely chopped

1 tsp cornflour

¹/₂ tsp chilli flakes

3 tbsp sesame oil

1 large head of broccoli, cut
   into florets

1 orange pepper, thinly sliced

1 red chilli, seeded and finely
   sliced

1 tbsp chilli oil, to taste

1 tbsp chopped fresh
   coriander, to garnish

method

1 Mix the beef strips with 1 tablespoon of the sesame seeds in a small bowl. In a separate bowl, whisk together the beef stock, soy sauce, ginger, garlic, cornflour and chilli flakes.

2 Heat 1 tablespoon of the sesame oil in a large frying pan or wok. Stir-fry the beef strips for 2–3 minutes. Remove and set aside.

3 Discard any oil left in the pan, then wipe with kitchen paper to remove any stray sesame seeds. Heat the remaining oil, add the broccoli, orange pepper, chilli and chilli oil, if using, and stir-fry for 2–3 minutes. Stir in the beef stock mixture, cover and simmer for 2 minutes.

4 Return the beef to the frying pan and simmer until the juices thicken, stirring occasionally. Cook for another 1–2 minutes.

5 Sprinkle with the remaining sesame seeds. Serve garnished with chopped coriander.

stir-fried beef with broccoli & ginger

ingredients

SERVES 4–6

350 g/12 oz fillet steak, cut
　　into thin strips
175 g/6 oz head of broccoli,
　　cut into florets
2 tbsp vegetable or peanut oil
1 garlic clove, finely chopped
1 tsp finely chopped
　　fresh ginger
1 small onion, finely sliced
1 tsp salt
1 tsp light soy sauce

marinade

1 tbsp light soy sauce
1 tsp sesame oil
1 tsp Shaoxing rice wine
1 tsp sugar
pinch of white pepper

method

1 Combine the marinade ingredients in a bowl, then mix in the beef. Cover and set aside for 1 hour, basting occasionally. Blanch the broccoli in a large saucepan of boiling water for 30 seconds. Drain and set aside.

2 In a preheated wok or deep saucepan, heat 1 tablespoon of the oil and stir-fry the garlic, ginger and onion for 1 minute. Add the broccoli and stir-fry for a further minute. Remove from the wok and set aside.

3 In the clean preheated wok or deep saucepan, heat the remaining oil and stir-fry the beef until it has changed colour. Return the broccoli mixture to the saucepan with the salt and light soy sauce and stir until cooked through. Serve immediately.

ginger beef
with yellow peppers

ingredients

SERVES 4

500 g/1 lb 2 oz beef fillet, cut
    into 2.5-cm/1-inch cubes
2 tsp peanut oil
2 garlic cloves, crushed
2 tbsp grated fresh ginger
pinch of chilli flakes
2 yellow peppers, thinly sliced
125 g/4^1/$_2$ oz baby corn
175 g/6 oz mangetout
hot noodles drizzled with
    sesame oil, to serve

marinade

2 tbsp soy sauce
2 tsp peanut oil
1^1/$_2$ tsp caster sugar
1 tsp cornflour

method

1 To make the marinade, mix the soy sauce,
peanut oil, sugar and cornflour in a bowl. Stir
in the beef cubes, then cover with clingfilm
and set aside to marinate for 30 minutes.

2 Heat the peanut oil in a frying pan or wok
over a medium heat. Add the garlic, ginger
and chilli flakes and cook for 30 seconds.
Stir in the yellow peppers and baby corn, and
stir-fry for 2 minutes. Add the mangetout and
cook for another minute.

3 Remove the vegetables from the frying pan.
Put the beef cubes and marinade into the
frying pan and stir-fry for 3–4 minutes or until
cooked to taste. Return the vegetables to the
frying pan, mix well and cook until all the
ingredients are heated through. Remove from
the heat and serve over noodles.

xinjiang rice pot with lamb

ingredients

SERVES 6–8

2 tbsp vegetable or peanut oil

300 g/10$\frac{1}{2}$ oz lamb or mutton,
   cut into bite-sized cubes

2 carrots, roughly chopped

2 onions, roughly chopped

1 tsp salt

1 tsp ground ginger

1 tsp Szechuan peppers,
   lightly roasted and lightly
   crushed

450 g/1 lb short- or medium-
   grain rice

850 ml/1$\frac{1}{2}$ pints water

method

1 In a large casserole, heat the oil and stir-fry the meat for 1–2 minutes, or until the pieces are sealed on all sides. Add the carrot and onion and stir-fry until the vegetables are beginning to soften. Add the salt, ginger and Szechuan peppers and mix well.

2 Finally, add the rice and water and bring to the boil. Cover the pan and cook over a low heat for 30 minutes, or until the rice has absorbed all the water. Serve alone or as part of a meal.

xinjiang lamb casserole

ingredients

SERVES 5-6

1–2 tbsp vegetable or
   peanut oil

400 g/14 oz lamb or mutton,
   cut into bite-sized cubes

1 onion, roughly chopped

1 green pepper, roughly
   chopped

1 carrot, roughly chopped

1 turnip, roughly chopped

2 tomatoes, roughly chopped

2.5-cm/1-inch piece of fresh
   ginger, finely sliced

300 ml/10 fl oz water

1 tsp salt

method

1 In a preheated wok or deep saucepan, heat the oil and stir-fry the lamb for 1–2 minutes, or until the meat is sealed on all sides.

2 Transfer the meat to a large casserole and add all the other ingredients. Bring to the boil, then cover and simmer over a low heat for 35 minutes.

spicy szechuan pork

ingredients

SERVES 4

280 g/10 oz pork belly,
    thinly sliced

1 tbsp vegetable or peanut oil

1 tbsp chilli bean sauce

1 tbsp fermented black beans,
    rinsed and lightly mashed

1 tsp sweet red bean paste
    (optional)

1 green pepper, finely sliced

1 red pepper, finely sliced

1 tsp sugar

1 tsp dark soy sauce

pinch of white pepper

method

1 Bring a saucepan of water to the boil and place the pork slices in the pan, then cover and simmer for about 20 minutes, skimming occasionally. Let the pork cool and rest before slicing thinly.

2 In a preheated wok or deep saucepan, heat the oil and stir-fry the pork slices until they begin to shrink. Stir in the chilli bean sauce, then add the black beans and the red bean paste, if using. Finally, toss in the peppers and the remaining ingredients and stir-fry for a couple of minutes.

szechuan-style pork & pepper

ingredients

SERVES 4

500 g/1 lb 2 oz pork fillet,
    cubed

2 tbsp cornflour

3 tbsp soy sauce

1 tbsp white wine vinegar

250 ml/9 fl oz water

2 tbsp peanut oil

2 leeks, thinly sliced

1 red pepper, cut into thin
    strips

1 courgette, cut into thin
    strips

1 carrot, cut into thin strips

pinch of salt

freshly cooked white and wild
    rice, to serve

marinade

1 tbsp soy sauce

pinch of chilli flakes

method

1 To make the marinade, mix the soy sauce and chilli flakes in a bowl. Add the pork cubes and toss to coat. Cover with clingfilm and set aside for 30 minutes.

2 Combine the cornflour, soy sauce and white wine vinegar in a small bowl. Stir in the water gradually, then set aside.

3 Heat 1 tablespoon of the oil in a wok or frying pan. Add the pork and marinade mixture and stir-fry for 2–3 minutes. Remove the pork from the frying pan with a slotted spoon and set aside.

4 Heat the remaining oil in the frying pan, add the leeks and red pepper and stir-fry for 2 minutes. Then add the courgette, carrot and salt and stir-fry for a further 2 minutes.

5 Stir in the pork and the cornflour mixture and bring to the boil, stirring constantly until the sauce thickens. Remove from the heat and serve immediately with freshly cooked white and wild rice.

spare ribs in a sweet-&-sour sauce

ingredients

SERVES 4

450 g/1 lb spare ribs, cut into
    bite-sized pieces (you or
    your butcher can cut ribs
    into pieces with a cleaver)
vegetable or peanut oil, for
    deep-frying

marinade
2 tsp light soy sauce
$^1/_2$ tsp salt
pinch of white pepper

sauce
3 tbsp white rice vinegar
2 tbsp sugar
1 tbsp light soy sauce
1 tbsp tomato ketchup
$1^1/_2$ tbsp vegetable or
    peanut oil
1 green pepper,
    roughly chopped
1 small onion,
    roughly chopped
1 small carrot, finely sliced
$^1/_2$ tsp finely chopped garlic
$^1/_2$ tsp finely chopped ginger
100 g/$3^1/_2$ oz pineapple chunks

method

1 Combine the marinade ingredients in a bowl, add the pork and marinate for at least 20 minutes.

2 Heat enough oil for deep-frying in a wok, deep-fat fryer, or large heavy-based saucepan to 180–190°C/350–375°F, or until a cube of bread browns in 30 seconds. Deep-fry the spare ribs for 8 minutes. Drain and set aside.

3 To prepare the sauce, first mix together the vinegar, sugar, light soy sauce and ketchup. Set aside.

4 In a preheated wok or deep saucepan, heat 1 tablespoon of the oil and stir-fry the pepper, onion and carrot for 2 minutes. Remove and set aside.

5 In the clean preheated wok or deep saucepan, heat the remaining oil and stir-fry the garlic and ginger until fragrant. Add the vinegar mixture. Bring back to the boil and add the pineapple chunks. Finally add the spare ribs and the pepper, onion and carrot. Stir until warmed through and serve immediately.

sweet-&-sour chicken

ingredients

SERVES 4–6

450 g/1 lb lean chicken meat, cubed

5 tbsp vegetable or peanut oil

$1/2$ tsp minced garlic

$1/2$ tsp finely chopped fresh ginger

1 green pepper, roughly chopped

1 onion, roughly chopped

1 carrot, finely sliced

1 tsp sesame oil

1 tbsp finely chopped spring onions

marinade

2 tsp light soy sauce

1 tsp Shaoxing rice wine

pinch of white pepper

$1/2$ tsp salt

dash of sesame oil

sauce

8 tbsp rice vinegar

4 tbsp sugar

2 tsp light soy sauce

6 tbsp tomato ketchup

method

1 Place all the marinade ingredients in a bowl and marinate the chicken cubes for at least 20 minutes.

2 To prepare the sauce, heat the vinegar in a saucepan and add the sugar, light soy sauce and tomato ketchup. Stir to dissolve the sugar, then set aside.

3 In a preheated wok or deep saucepan, heat 3 tablespoons of the oil and stir-fry the chicken until it starts to turn golden brown. Remove and set aside.

4 In the clean wok or deep saucepan, heat the remaining oil and cook the garlic and ginger until fragrant. Add the vegetables and cook for 2 minutes. Add the chicken and cook for 1 minute or until the chicken is thoroughly cooked. Finally add the sauce and sesame oil, then stir in the spring onions and serve.

gong bao chicken

ingredients

SERVES 4

2 boneless chicken breasts,
  with or without skin, cut
  into 1-cm/$^1/_2$-inch cubes

1 tbsp vegetable or peanut oil

10 dried red chillies or more,
  to taste, snipped into 2 or
  3 pieces

1 tsp Szechuan peppers

3 garlic cloves, finely sliced

2.5-cm/1-inch piece of fresh
  ginger, finely sliced

1 tbsp roughly chopped
  spring onions, white part
  only

85 g/3 oz peanuts, roasted

marinade

2 tsp light soy sauce

1 tsp Shaoxing rice wine

$^1/_2$ tsp sugar

sauce

1 tsp light soy sauce

1 tsp dark soy sauce

1 tsp black Chinese
  rice vinegar

a few drops of sesame oil

2 tbsp chicken stock

1 tsp sugar

method

1 Combine all the ingredients for the marinade in a bowl and marinate the chicken, covered, for at least 20 minutes. Combine all the ingredients for the sauce and set aside.

2 In a preheated wok or deep saucepan, heat the oil and stir-fry the chillies and peppers until crisp and fragrant. Toss in the chicken pieces. When they begin to turn white, add the garlic, ginger and spring onions. Stir-fry for about 5 minutes, or until the chicken is cooked.

3 Pour in the sauce, and when everything is well mixed, stir in the peanuts. Serve immediately.

bang bang chicken

ingredients

SERVES 4

350 g/12 oz boneless,
    skinless chicken meat

few drops of sesame oil

2 tbsp sesame paste

1 tbsp light soy sauce

1 tbsp chicken stock

$^1/_2$ tsp salt

pinch of sugar

8 tbsp shredded lettuce leaves
    and 1 tbsp sesame seeds,
    roasted, to serve

method

1 Place the chicken in a saucepan of cold water, then bring to the boil and simmer for 8–10 minutes. Drain and cool a little, then cut or tear the chicken into bite-sized pieces.

2 Mix together the sesame oil, sesame paste, light soy sauce, chicken stock, salt and sugar and whisk until the sauce is thick and smooth. Toss in the chicken.

3 To serve, put the shredded lettuce on a large plate and spoon the chicken and sauce on top. Sprinkle with the sesame seeds and serve at room temperature.

chicken with cashew nuts

ingredients

SERVES 4–6

450 g/1 lb boneless chicken
    meat, cut into bite-sized
    pieces

3 dried Chinese mushrooms,
    soaked in warm water for
    20 minutes

2 tbsp vegetable or peanut oil

4 slices of fresh ginger

1 tsp finely chopped garlic

1 red pepper, cut into
    2.5-cm/1-inch squares

1 tbsp light soy sauce

85 g/3 oz cashew nuts,
    roasted

marinade

3 tbsp light soy sauce

1 tsp Shaoxing rice wine

pinch of sugar

$1/2$ tsp salt

method

1 Combine all the ingredients for the marinade in a bowl and marinate the chicken, covered, for at least 20 minutes.

2 Squeeze any excess water from the mushrooms and finely slice, discarding any tough stems. Reserve the soaking water.

3 In a preheated wok or deep saucepan, heat 1 tablespoon of the oil. Add the ginger and stir-fry until fragrant. Stir in the chicken and cook for 2 minutes, or until it begins to turn brown. Before the chicken is cooked through, remove and set aside.

4 In the clean wok or deep saucepan, heat the remaining oil and stir-fry the garlic until fragrant. Add the mushrooms and red pepper and stir-fry for 1 minute. Add about 2 tablespoons of the mushroom soaking water and cook for about 2 minutes, or until the water has evaporated. Return the chicken to the wok, then add the light soy sauce and cashew nuts and stir-fry for 2 minutes, or until the chicken is thoroughly cooked through.

ginger chicken with toasted sesame seeds

ingredients

SERVES 4

500 g/1 lb 2 oz chicken
    breasts, skinned,
    cut into strips
2 tbsp peanut oil
1 leek, thinly sliced
1 head of broccoli, cut
    into small florets
2 carrots, thinly sliced
$1/2$ cauliflower, cut into
    small florets
1 tsp grated fresh ginger
5 tbsp white wine
2 tbsp sesame seeds
1 tbsp cornflour
1 tbsp water
freshly cooked rice, to serve

marinade
4 tbsp soy sauce
4 tbsp water

method

1 In a medium dish, combine the soy sauce with 4 tablespoons of water. Toss and coat the chicken strips in the sauce. Cover the dish with clingfilm and chill in the refrigerator for 1 hour.

2 Remove the chicken from the marinade with a slotted spoon. Heat the oil in a frying pan or wok and stir-fry the chicken and leek until the chicken is browned and the leek is beginning to soften. Stir in the vegetables, ginger and wine. Reduce the heat, cover and simmer for 5 minutes.

3 Place the sesame seeds on a baking sheet under a hot grill. Stir them once to make sure they toast evenly. Set aside to cool.

4 In a small bowl, combine the cornflour with 1 tablespoon of water and whisk until smooth. Gradually add the liquid to the frying pan, stirring constantly until thickened.

5 Pile onto a bed of freshly cooked rice, top with the sesame seeds and serve.

chinese crispy duck

ingredients

SERVES 4

3 tbsp soy sauce

$1/4$ tsp Chinese five-spice
    powder

$1/4$ tsp pepper and pinch
    of salt

4 duck legs or breasts,
    cut into pieces

3 tbsp vegetable oil

1 tsp dark sesame oil

1 tsp finely chopped
    fresh ginger

1 large garlic clove,
    finely chopped

4 spring onions, white part
    thickly sliced, green part
    shredded

2 tbsp rice wine or dry sherry

1 tbsp oyster sauce

3 whole star anise

2 tsp black peppercorns

450–600 ml/16 fl oz–1 pint
    chicken stock or water

6 dried shiitake mushrooms,
    soaked in warm water for
    20 minutes

225 g/8 oz canned water
    chestnuts, drained

2 tbsp cornflour

method

1 Combine 1 tablespoon of the soy sauce, the five-spice powder, pepper and salt and rub over the duck pieces. Place $2^1/2$ tablespoons of vegetable oil in a flameproof casserole, add the duck pieces and cook until browned, then transfer to a plate and set aside.

2 Drain the fat from the casserole and wipe out. Add the sesame oil and remaining vegetable oil and heat. Add the ginger and garlic and cook for a few seconds. Add the sliced white spring onions and cook for a few more seconds. Return the duck to the casserole. Add the rice wine, oyster sauce, star anise, peppercorns and remaining soy sauce. Pour in enough stock to just cover the duck. Bring to the boil, cover and simmer gently for $1^1/2$ hours, adding more stock if necessary.

3 Drain the mushrooms and squeeze dry. Slice the caps, add to the duck with the water chestnuts, and simmer for a further 20 minutes.

4 Mix the cornflour with 2 tablespoons of the cooking liquid to form a smooth paste. Add to the remaining liquid, stirring, until thickened. To serve, garnish with shredded green spring onions.

peking duck

ingredients

SERVES 6–10

1 duck, weighing 2 kg/
    4 lb 8 oz

1.7 litres/3 pints boiling water

1 tbsp honey

1 tbsp Shaoxing rice wine

1 tsp white rice vinegar

1 cucumber, peeled,
    deseeded and julienned

10 spring onions, white part
    only, shredded

30 Peking duck pancakes

plum or hoisin sauce, or both

method

1 To prepare the duck, massage the skin to separate it from the meat.

2 Pour the boiling water into a large saucepan, then add the honey, Shaoxing and vinegar and lower in the duck. Baste for about 1 minute. Remove the duck and hang it to dry for a few hours or overnight.

3 Preheat the oven to 200°C/400°F/Gas Mark 5. Place the duck on a rack above a roasting tin and roast for at least 1 hour, or until the skin is very crispy and the duck cooked through.

4 To serve, bring the duck to the table, together with the cucumber, spring onions and pancakes, and carve off the skin first. On a pancake, arrange a little skin with some cucumber and spring onion pieces. Top with a little plum or hoisin sauce, or both. Roll up and eat. Repeat the process with the lean meat.

fried fish with pine kernels

ingredients

SERVES 4–6

1/2 tsp salt

450 g/1 lb thick white fish
fillets, cut into 2.5-cm/
1-inch cubes

2 dried Chinese mushrooms,
soaked in warm water
for 20 minutes

3 tbsp vegetable or peanut oil

2.5-cm/1-inch piece of fresh
ginger, finely shredded

1 tbsp chopped spring onions

1 red pepper, cut into
2.5-cm/1-inch squares

1 green pepper, cut into
2.5-cm/1-inch squares

25 g/1 oz fresh or canned
bamboo shoots, rinsed
and cut into small cubes
(if using fresh shoots,
boil in water first for
30 minutes)

2 tsp Shaoxing rice wine

2 tbsp pine kernels, toasted

method

1 Sprinkle the salt over the fish and set aside
for 20 minutes. Squeeze out any excess water
from the mushrooms and finely slice, discarding
any tough stems.

2 In a preheated wok, heat 2 tablespoons of
the oil and fry the fish for 3 minutes. Drain
and set aside.

3 In a clean, preheated wok, heat the remaining
oil and toss in the ginger. Stir until fragrant,
then add the spring onions, peppers, bamboo
shoots, mushrooms and Shaoxing and cook
for 1–2 minutes.

4 Finally add the fish and stir to warm through.
Sprinkle with the pine kernels and serve.

chillies stuffed with fish paste

ingredients

SERVES 4–6

225 g/8 oz white fish, minced

2 tbsp lightly beaten egg

4–6 mild red and green
    chillies

vegetable or peanut oil, for
    shallow-frying

2 garlic cloves, finely chopped

1/2 tsp fermented black beans,
    rinsed and lightly mashed

1 tbsp light soy sauce

pinch of sugar

1 tbsp water

marinade

1 tsp finely chopped
    fresh ginger

pinch of salt

pinch of white pepper

1/2 tsp vegetable or peanut oil

method

1 Combine all the ingredients for the marinade
in a bowl and marinate the fish for 20 minutes.
Add the egg and mix by hand to create a
smooth paste.

2 To prepare the chillies, cut in half lengthways
and scoop out the seeds and loose flesh. Cut
into bite-sized pieces. Spread each piece of
chilli with about 1/2 teaspoon of the fish paste.

3 In a preheated wok or deep saucepan, heat
plenty of the oil and cook the chilli pieces on
both sides until beginning to turn golden brown.
Drain and set aside.

4 Heat 1 tablespoon of the oil in a wok or deep
saucepan and stir-fry the garlic until aromatic.
Stir in the black beans and mix well. Add the
light soy sauce and sugar and stir, then add
the chilli pieces. Add the water, then cover
and simmer over a low heat for 5 minutes.
Serve immediately.

whole deep-fried fish with soy & ginger

ingredients

SERVES 4–5

6 dried Chinese mushrooms, soaked in warm water for 20 minutes

3 tbsp rice vinegar

2 tbsp brown sugar

3 tbsp dark soy sauce

7.5-cm/3-inch piece fresh ginger, finely chopped

4 spring onions, sliced diagonally

2 tsp cornflour

2 tbsp lime juice

1 sea bass, cleaned and scaled, about 1 kg/ 2 lb 4 oz

4 tbsp plain flour

sunflower oil, for deep-frying

salt and pepper

shredded Napa cabbage and radish slices, to serve

1 radish, sliced but left whole, to garnish

method

1 Drain the mushrooms, reserving 100 ml/ 3$\frac{1}{2}$ fl oz of the liquid. Cut the mushrooms into thin slices. Mix the reserved mushroom liquid with the vinegar, sugar and soy sauce. Put in a saucepan with the mushrooms and bring to the boil. Reduce the heat and simmer for 3–4 minutes. Add the ginger and spring onions and simmer for 1 minute.

2 Blend the cornflour and lime juice, stir into the pan, and cook, stirring, for 1–2 minutes until the sauce thickens and clears. Set aside.

3 Season the fish inside and out with salt and pepper, then dust lightly with flour.

4 Heat 2.5 cm/1 inch of oil in a wide, heavy-based saucepan to 180–190°C/350–375°F, or until a cube of bread browns in 30 seconds. Lower the fish carefully into the oil and deep-fry on one side for 3–4 minutes until golden brown. Use 2 metal spatulas to turn the fish carefully and deep-fry on the other side for a further 3–4 minutes, until golden brown.

5 Remove the fish, drain off the excess oil and put on a serving plate. Reheat the sauce until boiling, then spoon it over the fish. Serve immediately with shredded Napa cabbage and sliced radishes, garnished with the radish.

five-willow fish

ingredients

SERVES 4–6

1 whole sea bass or similar,
    weighing 450–650 g/
    1 lb–1 lb 7 oz, gutted

2 tsp salt

6 tbsp vegetable or peanut oil

2 slices fresh ginger

2 garlic cloves, finely sliced

2 spring onions, roughly
    chopped

1 green pepper, thinly sliced

1 red pepper, thinly sliced

1 carrot, finely sliced

55 g/2 oz fresh or canned
    bamboo shoots, rinsed
    and thinly sliced (if using
    fresh shoots, boil in water
    first for 30 minutes)

2 tomatoes, peeled, deseeded
    and thinly sliced

1 tbsp Shaoxing rice wine

2 tbsp white rice vinegar

1 tbsp light soy sauce

1 tbsp sugar

method

1 To prepare the fish, clean and dry it thoroughly. Score the fish on both sides with deep, diagonal cuts. Press $1/2$ teaspoon of the salt into the skin.

2 In a preheated wok or deep saucepan, heat 4 tablespoons of the oil and cook the fish for about 4 minutes on each side, or until the flesh is soft. Drain, then set aside and keep warm.

3 In a preheated wok or deep saucepan, heat the remaining oil and stir-fry the ginger, garlic and spring onions until fragrant. Toss in the vegetables with the remaining salt and stir rapidly for 2–3 minutes. Add the remaining ingredients and cook, mixing well, for 2–3 minutes. Pour the sauce over the fish and serve immediately.

steamed sole with black bean sauce

ingredients

SERVES 3–4

1 sole, gutted

1/2 tsp salt

2 tsp fermented black beans, rinsed and chopped

2 tsp finely chopped garlic

1 tsp finely shredded fresh ginger

1 tbsp shredded spring onions

1 tbsp light soy sauce

1 tsp Shaoxing rice wine

1 tsp vegetable or peanut oil

dash of sesame oil

1/2 tsp sugar

pinch of white pepper

method

1 Place the fish on a plate or create a small dish with foil.

2 Arrange all the other ingredients on top of the fish. Place in a steamer for about 10–12 minutes, or until the fish is cooked through.

deep-fried river fish with chilli bean sauce

ingredients

SERVES 4–6

1 whole freshwater fish, such
    as trout or carp, weighing
    400 g/14 oz, gutted
1 heaped tbsp plain flour
pinch of salt
100 ml/3½ fl oz water
vegetable or peanut oil,
    for deep-frying

sauce

1 tsp dried chilli flakes
100 ml/3½ fl oz vegetable or
    peanut oil
1 garlic clove, finely chopped
1 tsp finely chopped fresh
    ginger
1 tbsp chilli bean sauce
½ tsp white pepper
2 tsp sugar
1 tbsp white rice vinegar
1 tsp finely chopped spring
    onions

method

1 To prepare the fish, clean and dry thoroughly. Mix together the flour, salt and water to create a light batter. Coat the fish.

2 Heat enough oil for deep-frying in a wok, deep-fat fryer, or large heavy-based saucepan to 180–190°C/350–375°F, or until a cube of bread browns in 30 seconds. Deep-fry the fish until the skin is crisp and golden brown. Drain, then set aside and keep warm.

3 To make the sauce, put the dried chilli flakes in a heatproof dish. Heat all but 1 tablespoon of the oil in a small saucepan and, when smoking, pour over the dried chilli flakes. Set aside.

4 In a preheated wok or deep saucepan, heat the remaining oil and stir-fry the garlic and ginger until fragrant. Stir in the chilli bean sauce, then add the oil and chilli flake mixture. Season with the pepper, sugar and vinegar. Turn off the heat and stir in the spring onions. Tip over the fish and serve immediately.

simple stir-fried scallops

ingredients

SERVES 4

450 g/1 lb scallops

2 tbsp sesame oil

1 tbsp chopped fresh
    coriander

1 tbsp chopped fresh flat-leaf
    parsley

rice noodles, to serve

sauce

2 tbsp lemon juice

2 tbsp soy sauce

1 tbsp honey

1 tbsp minced fresh ginger

1 tbsp fish sauce

1 clove garlic, peeled and
    flattened

method

1 Combine the lemon juice, soy sauce, honey, ginger, fish sauce and garlic in a bowl and stir well to dissolve the honey. Add the scallops and toss to coat.

2 Heat a heavy frying pan or wok over the highest heat for 3 minutes. Add the oil and heat for 30 seconds.

3 Add the scallops with their sauce and the coriander and parsley to the pan. Stir constantly, cooking for about 3 minutes (less time if the scallops are small). Serve immediately with rice noodles.

stir-fried scallops
with asparagus

ingredients

SERVES 4

225 g/8 oz scallops

2 tsp salt

225 g/8 oz asparagus

3 tbsp vegetable or peanut oil

55 g/2 oz fresh or canned
   bamboo shoots, rinsed
   and thinly sliced (if using
   fresh shoots, boil in water
   first for 30 minutes)

1 small carrot, finely sliced

4 thin slices of fresh ginger

pinch of white pepper

2 tbsp Shaoxing rice wine

2 tbsp chicken stock

1 tsp sesame oil

method

1 Sprinkle the scallops with 1 teaspoon of the salt and set aside for 20 minutes.

2 Trim the asparagus, discarding the tough ends. Cut into 5-cm/2-inch pieces and blanch in a large saucepan of boiling water for 30 seconds. Drain and set aside.

3 In a preheated wok, heat 1 tablespoon of the oil and cook the scallops for 30 seconds. Drain and set aside.

4 In the clean wok, heat another tablespoon of the oil and stir-fry the asparagus, bamboo shoots and carrot for 2 minutes. Season with the remaining salt. Drain and set aside.

5 In the clean wok, heat the remaining oil, then add the ginger and stir-fry until fragrant. Return the scallops and vegetables to the wok and sprinkle with the pepper, Shaoxing and stock. Cover and continue cooking for 2 minutes, then toss through the sesame oil and serve.

clams in black bean sauce

ingredients

SERVES 4

900 g/2 lb small clams

1 tbsp vegetable or peanut oil

1 tsp finely chopped
    fresh ginger

1 tsp finely chopped garlic

1 tbsp fermented black beans,
    rinsed and roughly
    chopped

2 tsp Shaoxing rice wine

1 tbsp finely chopped
    spring onions

1 tsp salt (optional)

method

1 Start by washing the clams thoroughly, then soak them in clean water until needed.

2 In a preheated wok or deep saucepan, heat the oil and stir-fry the ginger and garlic until fragrant. Add the black beans and cook for 1 minute.

3 Over a high heat, add the drained clams and Shaoxing and stir-fry for 2 minutes to mix everything together. Cover and cook for about 3 minutes. Add the spring onions and salt, if necessary, and serve immediately.

ginger prawns with oyster mushrooms

ingredients

SERVES 4

about 3 tbsp vegetable oil

3 carrots, thinly sliced

350 g/12 oz oyster
  mushrooms, thinly sliced

1 large red pepper, thinly
  sliced

450 g/1 lb large prawns,
  peeled

2 garlic cloves, crushed

fresh coriander leaves,
  to garnish

sauce

150 ml/5 fl oz chicken stock

2 tsp sesame seeds

3 tsp grated fresh ginger

1 tbsp soy sauce

1/4 tsp hot pepper sauce

1 tsp cornflour

method

1 In a small bowl, stir together the chicken stock, sesame seeds, ginger, soy sauce, hot pepper sauce and cornflour until well blended. Set aside.

2 In a large frying pan or wok, heat 2 tablespoons of the oil. Stir-fry the carrots for 3 minutes, then remove from the pan and set aside.

3 Add another 1 tablespoon of the oil to the frying pan and fry the mushrooms for 2 minutes. Remove from the pan and set aside.

4 Add more oil if needed and stir-fry the pepper with the prawns and garlic for 3 minutes, until the prawns turn pink and opaque.

5 Stir the sauce again and pour it into the frying pan. Cook until the mixture bubbles, then return the carrots and mushrooms to the pan. Cover and cook for a further 2 minutes, until heated through. Serve garnished with coriander.

prawns, mangetout & cashew nuts

ingredients

SERVES 4

85 g/3 oz cashew nuts

3 tbsp peanut oil

4 spring onions, slivered

2 celery sticks, thinly sliced

3 carrots, finely sliced

100 g/3^{1}/$_{2}$ oz baby corn, halved

175 g/6 oz mushrooms, finely sliced

1 clove of garlic, roughly chopped

450 g/1 lb raw prawns, peeled

1 tsp cornflour

2 tbsp soy sauce

50 ml/2 fl oz chicken stock

225 g/8 oz Savoy cabbage, shredded

175 g/6 oz mangetout

freshly cooked rice, to serve

method

1 Put a frying pan or wok over a medium heat, add the cashew nuts and toast them until they begin to brown. Remove with a slotted spoon and set aside.

2 Add the oil to the frying pan and heat. Add the spring onions, celery, carrots and baby corn and cook, stirring occasionally, over a medium–high heat for 3–4 minutes.

3 Add the mushrooms and cook until they become brown. Mix in the garlic and prawns, stirring until the prawns turn pink.

4 Mix the cornflour with the soy sauce and chicken stock until smooth. Add the liquid to the prawn mixture and stir. Then add the Savoy cabbage, mangetout and all but a few of the cashew nuts and cook for 2 minutes.

5 Serve on a bed of rice, garnished with the reserved cashew nuts.

stir-fried fresh crab with ginger

ingredients

SERVES 4

3 tbsp vegetable or peanut oil

2 large fresh crabs, cleaned,
   broken into pieces and
   legs cracked with a cleaver

55 g/2 oz fresh ginger,
   julienned

100 g/3^1/$_2$ oz spring onions,
   chopped into 5-cm/2-inch
   lengths

2 tbsp light soy sauce

1 tsp sugar

pinch of white pepper

method

1 In a preheated wok or deep saucepan, heat 2 tablespoons of the oil and cook the crab over a high heat for 3–4 minutes. Remove and set aside.

2 In the clean wok or deep saucepan, heat the remaining oil, then toss in the ginger and stir until fragrant. Add the spring onions, then stir in the crab pieces. Add the light soy sauce, sugar and pepper. Cover and simmer for 1 minute, then serve immediately.

baby squid stuffed with pork and mushrooms

ingredients

SERVES 6-8

400 g/14 oz baby squid

4 dried Chinese mushrooms,
   soaked in warm water
   for 20 minutes

225 g/8 oz pork mince

4 water chestnuts,
   finely chopped

$^1/_2$ tsp sesame oil

1 tsp salt

$^1/_2$ tsp white pepper

dark soy sauce and 1 red
   Thai chilli, chopped
   (optional), to serve

method

1 Clean the squid thoroughly, removing all the tentacles. Squeeze out any excess water from the mushrooms and finely chop, discarding any tough stems.

2 Mix the mushrooms with the pork, water chestnuts, sesame oil, salt and pepper.

3 Force the stuffing into the squid, pressing firmly but leaving enough room to secure each one with a cocktail stick.

4 Steam for 15 minutes. Serve with a good soy sauce for dipping, adding the chilli, if you like.

sweet chilli squid

ingredients

SERVES 4

1 tbsp sesame seeds, toasted

2½ tbsp sesame oil

280 g/10 oz squid, cut into strips

2 red peppers, thinly sliced

3 shallots, thinly sliced

85 g/3 oz mushrooms, thinly sliced

1 tbsp dry sherry

4 tbsp soy sauce

1 tsp sugar

1 tsp hot chilli flakes, or to taste

1 clove of garlic, crushed

freshly cooked rice, to serve

method

1 Place the sesame seeds on a baking sheet, toast under a hot grill and set aside.

2 Heat 1 tablespoon of the oil in a frying pan or wok over a medium heat. Add the squid and cook for 2 minutes, then remove and set aside.

3 Add another 1 tablespoon of the oil to the frying pan and fry the peppers and shallots over a medium heat for 1 minute. Add the mushrooms and fry for a further 2 minutes.

4 Return the squid to the frying pan and add the sherry, soy sauce, sugar, chilli flakes and garlic, stirring thoroughly. Cook for a further 2 minutes.

5 Sprinkle with the toasted sesame seeds, drizzle over the remaining sesame oil and mix. Serve on a bed of freshly cooked rice.

noodles & rice

Noodles and rice are the two staple carbohydrate foods of China. Rice is traditionally grown and eaten in the southern part of the country, while grains such as wheat and millet are associated with the north. The wheat is transformed into noodles, usually made with eggs, which come in all shapes and sizes and are available either fresh or dried. Rice is cooked simply as it is, but is also made into noodles, either flat ones, known as rice sticks, or very thin rice vermicelli. These are an excellent substitute for wheat-based noodles if you suffer a gluten intolerance.

There are some very poetic names for Chinese noodle recipes – Ants Climbing a Tree and Cross the Bridge Noodles are both worth making, if only to see the looks on the faces of family and friends as you serve these intriguing and very tasty dishes! Using noodles in different ways is also fun – noodle baskets are easy to master and look great filled with Chicken Chow Mein, and Sweet & Sour Vegetables on Noodle Pancakes are fabulous, too.

Fried rice is one of those dishes everyone loves, and there are several options in this section, including Fried Rice with Pork & Prawns, a flavourful combination of meat and seafood, and Chicken Fried Rice – perfect fast food for any time of the day.

beef noodles
with oyster sauce

ingredients

SERVES 4

300 g/10^{1}/$_{2}$ oz boneless
   sirloin steak, thinly sliced

250 g/9 oz dried thick
   Chinese egg noodles

2 tbsp peanut or corn oil

225 g/8 oz fresh asparagus
   spears, woody ends cut
   off, chopped

2 large garlic cloves, finely
   chopped

1-cm/^{1}/$_{2}$-inch piece fresh
   ginger, peeled and finely
   chopped

^{1}/$_{2}$ red onion, thinly sliced

4 tbsp beef or vegetable stock

1^{1}/$_{2}$ tbsp rice wine

2–3 tbsp bottled oyster sauce

toasted sesame seeds,
   to garnish

marinade

1 tbsp light soy sauce

1 tsp toasted sesame oil

2 tsp rice wine

method

1 To make the marinade, stir the ingredients together in a non-metallic bowl. Stir in the steak so all the slices are coated, then set aside to marinate for at least 15 minutes.

2 Meanwhile, boil the noodles in a saucepan of boiling water for 4 minutes, or according to the packet instructions, until soft. Drain, rinse and drain again, then set aside.

3 When you are ready to stir-fry, heat a wok or large frying pan over a high heat. Add 1 tablespoon of the oil and heat. Add the asparagus and stir-fry for 1 minute. Tip the beef and marinade into the wok, standing back because it will splutter, and continue stir-frying until the beef is cooked to your taste, about 1^{1}/$_{2}$ minutes for medium. Remove the beef and asparagus from the wok and set aside.

4 Heat the remaining oil and stir-fry the garlic, ginger and onion for about 1 minute, until the onion is soft. Add the stock, rice wine and oyster sauce and bring to the boil, stirring. Return the beef and asparagus to the wok, along with the noodles. Use 2 forks to mix all the ingredients together and stir around until the noodles are hot. Sprinkle with toasted sesame seeds.

rice sticks with beef in black bean sauce

ingredients

SERVES 4–6

225 g/8 oz rump steak,
    finely sliced

225 g/8 oz rice sticks

2–3 tbsp vegetable or
    peanut oil

1 small onion, finely sliced

1 green pepper, finely sliced

1 red pepper, finely sliced

2 tbsp black bean sauce

2–3 tbsp light soy sauce

marinade

1 tbsp dark soy sauce

1 tsp Shaoxing rice wine

1/2 tsp sugar

1/2 tsp white pepper

method

1 Combine all the marinade ingredients in a bowl, add the beef and marinate for at least 20 minutes.

2 Cook the rice sticks according to the directions on the packet. When cooked, drain and set aside.

3 In a preheated wok or deep saucepan, heat the oil and stir-fry the beef for 1 minute, or until the meat has changed colour. Drain the meat and set aside.

4 Pour off any excess oil from the wok and stir-fry the onion and peppers for 1 minute. Add the black bean sauce and stir well, then pour in the light soy sauce. Toss the rice sticks in the vegetables and when fully incorporated, add the beef and stir until warmed through. Serve immediately.

ants climbing a tree

ingredients

SERVES 4

250 g/9 oz dried thick
rice noodles

1 tbsp cornflour

3 tbsp soy sauce

1½ tbsp rice wine

1½ tsp sugar

1½ tsp toasted sesame oil

350 g/12 oz lean fresh
pork mince

1½ tbsp peanut or toasted
sesame oil

2 large garlic cloves, finely
chopped

1 large fresh red chilli, or to
taste, deseeded and thinly
sliced

3 spring onions, finely
chopped

finely chopped fresh
coriander or parsley,
to garnish

method

1 Soak the rice noodles in enough lukewarm water to cover for 20 minutes, until soft, or cook according to the packet instructions. Drain well and set aside.

2 Meanwhile, put the cornflour in another large bowl, then stir in the soy sauce, rice wine, sugar and sesame oil, stirring so that no lumps form. Add the pork mince and use your hands to toss the ingredients together without squeezing the pork; set aside to marinate for 10 minutes.

3 Heat a wok or large frying pan over a high heat. Add the oil and heat until it shimmers. Add the garlic, chilli and spring onions and stir around for about 30 seconds. Tip in the pork mince together with any marinade left in the bowl and stir-fry for about 5 minutes, or until the pork is no longer pink. Add the noodles and use 2 forks to mix together. Sprinkle with the chopped herbs and serve.

pork lo mein

ingredients

SERVES 4–6

175 g/6 oz boneless lean
    pork, shredded

225 g/8 oz egg noodles

1½ tbsp vegetable or
    peanut oil

2 tsp finely chopped garlic

1 tsp finely chopped
    fresh ginger

1 carrot, julienned

225 g/8 oz finely sliced
    mushrooms

1 green pepper, thinly sliced

1 tsp salt

125 ml/4 fl oz hot chicken
    stock

200 g/7 oz beansprouts,
    trimmed

2 tbsp finely chopped
    spring onions

marinade

1 tsp light soy sauce

dash of sesame oil

pinch of white pepper

method

1 Combine all the marinade ingredients in a
bowl, add the pork and marinate for at least
20 minutes.

2 Cook the noodles according to the packet
instructions. When cooked, drain and set aside.

3 In a preheated wok or deep saucepan, heat
1 teaspoon of the oil and stir-fry the pork until
it has changed colour. Remove and set aside.

4 In the clean wok or saucepan, heat the
remaining oil and stir-fry the garlic and ginger
until fragrant. Add the carrot and cook for
1 minute, then add the mushrooms and cook
for a further 1 minute. Toss in the pepper
and cook for 1 minute more. Add the pork,
salt and stock and heat through. Finally, toss
in the noodles, followed by the beansprouts,
and stir well. Sprinkle with the spring onions
and serve.

singapore noodles

ingredients

SERVES 4

200 g/7 oz dried rice
    vermicelli noodles

1 tbsp mild, medium or hot
    curry paste, to taste

1 tsp ground turmeric

6 tbsp water

2 tbsp peanut or corn oil

1/2 onion, very thinly sliced

2 large garlic cloves, thinly
    sliced

85 g/3 oz head of broccoli,
    cut into very small florets

85 g/3 oz green beans,
    trimmed, and cut into
    2.5-cm/1-inch pieces

85 g/3 oz pork fillet, cut in
    half lengthways, and then
    into thin strips, or skinless,
    boneless chicken breast,
    thinly sliced

85 g/3 oz small cooked peeled
    prawns, thawed if frozen

55 g/2 oz Chinese cabbage or
    romaine lettuce, thinly
    shredded

1/4 Thai chilli, or to taste,
    deseeded and thinly sliced

2 spring onions, light green
    parts only, thinly shredded

fresh coriander, to garnish

method

1 Soak the noodles in enough lukewarm water to cover for 20 minutes, or according to the packet instructions, until soft. Drain and set aside until required. While the noodles are soaking, put the curry paste and turmeric in a small bowl and stir in 4 tablespoons of the water, then set aside.

2 Heat a wok or large frying pan over a high heat. Add the oil and heat until it shimmers. Add the onion and garlic and stir-fry for 1 minute, or until the onion softens. Add the broccoli florets and beans to the wok with the remaining 2 tablespoons of water and continue stir-frying for 2 minutes. Add the pork and stir-fry for 1 more minute. Add the prawns, cabbage and chilli to the wok and continue stir-frying for a further 2 minutes, until the meat is cooked through and the vegetables are tender, but still with a little bite. Scoop out of the wok and keep warm.

3 Add the spring onions, noodles and curry paste mixture to the wok. Use 2 forks to mix the noodles and onions together, and continue stir-frying for about 2 minutes, until the noodles are hot and have picked up a dark golden colour from the turmeric. Return the other ingredients to the wok and continue stir-frying and mixing for 1 minute. Garnish with fresh coriander.

sour-&-spicy pork

ingredients

SERVES 4

55 g/2 oz dried Chinese
    cloud ear mushrooms,
    soaked in boiling water
    for 20 minutes

100 g/3¹/₂ oz baby corn,
    halved lengthways

2 tbsp honey

1 tbsp tamarind paste

4 tbsp boiling water

2 tbsp dark soy sauce

1 tbsp rice vinegar

2 tbsp peanut or corn oil

1 large garlic clove, very
    finely chopped

1-cm/¹/₂-inch piece fresh
    ginger, peeled and very
    finely chopped

¹/₂ tsp dried red pepper
    flakes, or to taste

350 g/12 oz pork fillet,
    thinly sliced

4 spring onions, thickly sliced
    diagonally

1 green pepper, cored,
    deseeded and sliced

250 g/9 oz fresh Hokkien
    noodles

chopped fresh coriander,
    to garnish

method

1 Drain the mushrooms well, then cut off and discard any thick stems, and slice the cups if they are large. Meanwhile, bring a large saucepan of lightly salted water to the boil, add the baby corn and blanch for 3 minutes. Drain the corn and run them under cold running water to stop the cooking, then set aside.

2 Put the honey and tamarind paste in a small bowl and stir in the water, stirring until the paste dissolves. Then stir in the soy sauce and rice vinegar and set aside.

3 Heat a wok or large frying pan over a high heat. Add 1 tablespoon of the oil and heat until it shimmers. Add the garlic, ginger and red pepper flakes and stir-fry for about 30 seconds. Add the pork and continue stir-frying for 2 minutes.

4 Add the remaining oil to the wok and heat. Add the spring onions, pepper, mushrooms and baby corn, along with the tamarind mixture, and stir-fry for a further 2–3 minutes, until the pork is cooked through and the vegetables are tender, but still firm to the bite. Add the noodles and use 2 forks to mix all the ingredients together. When the noodles and sauce are hot, sprinkle with coriander.

hoisin pork
with garlic noodles

ingredients

SERVES 4

250 g/9 oz dried thick Chinese
    egg noodles, or Chinese
    wholemeal egg noodles

450 g/1 lb pork fillet, thinly
    sliced

1 tsp sugar

1 tbsp peanut or corn oil

4 tbsp rice vinegar

4 tbsp white wine vinegar

4 tbsp bottled hoisin sauce

2 spring onions, sliced
    diagonally

about 2 tbsp garlic-flavoured
    corn oil

2 large garlic cloves, thinly
    sliced

method

1 Cook the noodles in a saucepan of boiling
water for 3 minutes, or according to the packet
instructions, until soft. Drain well, rinse under
cold water to stop the cooking and drain again,
then set aside.

2 Sprinkle the pork slices with the sugar and
use your hands to toss together. Heat a wok or
large frying pan over a high heat. Add the oil
and heat until it shimmers. Add the pork and
stir-fry for about 3 minutes, until the pork is
cooked through and is no longer pink. Use a
slotted spoon to remove the pork from the wok
and keep warm. Add both vinegars to the wok
and boil until they are reduced to about
5 tablespoons. Pour in the hoisin sauce with
the spring onions and let bubble until reduced
by half. Add to the pork and stir together.

3 Quickly wipe out the wok and reheat. Add the
garlic-flavoured oil and heat until it shimmers.
Add the garlic slices and stir around for about
30 seconds, until they are golden and crisp,
then use a slotted spoon to scoop them out of
the wok and set aside.

4 Add the noodles to the wok and stir to warm
through. Divide the noodles between 4 plates,
top with the pork and onion mixture and
sprinkle with cooked garlic slices.

fried rice with pork & prawns

ingredients

SERVES 4

3 tsp vegetable or peanut oil

1 egg, lightly beaten

100 g/3^1/$_2$ oz raw prawns, peeled, deveined and cut into 2 pieces

100 g/3^1/$_2$ oz cha siu (roast honeyed pork), finely chopped

2 tbsp finely chopped spring onions

200 g/7 oz cooked rice, chilled

1 tsp salt

method

1 In a preheated wok or deep saucepan, heat 1 teaspoon of the oil and pour in the egg. Cook until scrambled. Remove and set aside.

2 Add the remaining oil and stir-fry the prawns, cha siu and spring onions for about 2 minutes. Add the rice and salt, breaking up the rice into grains, and cook for a further 2 minutes. Finally, stir in the cooked egg. Serve immediately.

peking duck salad

ingredients

SERVES 4

1/2 Peking duck (see page
    86), or 2 duck breasts
450 g/1 lb fresh Hokkien
    noodles
5 tbsp bottled hoisin sauce
5 tbsp bottled plum sauce
1 small cucumber
4 spring onions, sliced
    diagonally

method

1 Roast and cool the duck breasts, if using.
Remove the crisp skin from the Peking duck
or roasted duck breasts and cut it into thin
strips, then slice the meat and set both aside
separately.

2 Rinse the noodles under lukewarm water to
separate them, then let them drain. Meanwhile,
mix the hoisin and plum sauces together in a
large bowl and add the noodles after any excess
water has dripped off. Add the duck skin to the
bowl and stir together.

3 Cut the cucumber in half lengthways, then
use a teaspoon to scoop out the seeds. Cut
into half-moon slices and add to the noodles.
Add the spring onions to the bowl. Use your
hands to mix all the ingredients together so
they are coated with the sauce.

4 Transfer the noodles to a large platter and
arrange the duck meat on top.

chicken fried rice

ingredients

SERVES 4

1/2 tbsp sesame oil

6 shallots, peeled and cut
    into quarters

450 g/1 lb cooked, cubed
    chicken meat

3 tbsp soy sauce

2 carrots, diced

1 celery stick, diced

1 red pepper, diced

175 g/6 oz fresh peas

100 g/3 1/2 oz canned
    sweetcorn

275 g/9 3/4 oz cooked
    long-grain rice

2 large eggs, scrambled

method

1 Heat the oil in a large frying pan over a medium heat. Add the shallots and fry until soft, then add the chicken and 2 tablespoons of the soy sauce and stir-fry for 5–6 minutes.

2 Stir in the carrots, celery, red pepper, peas and sweetcorn and stir-fry for a further 5 minutes. Add the rice and stir thoroughly.

3 Finally, stir in the scrambled eggs and the remaining tablespoon of soy sauce. Serve immediately.

sweet-&-sour noodles with chicken

ingredients

SERVES 4

250 g/9 oz dried medium
    Chinese egg noodles

2 tbsp peanut or corn oil

1 onion, thinly sliced

4 boneless chicken thighs,
    skinned and cut into
    thin strips

1 carrot, peeled and cut into
    thin half-moon slices

1 red pepper, cored,
    deseeded and finely
    chopped

100 g/3$^{1}/_{2}$ oz canned bamboo
    shoots, drained weight

55 g/2 oz cashew nuts

sweet-&-sour sauce

125 ml/4 fl oz water

1$^{1}/_{2}$ teaspoons arrowroot

4 tbsp rice vinegar

3 tbsp brown sugar

2 tsp dark soy sauce

2 tsp tomato purée

2 large garlic cloves, very
    finely chopped

1-cm/$^{1}/_{2}$-inch piece fresh
    ginger, peeled and very
    finely chopped

pinch of salt

method

1 Cook the noodles in a large saucepan of boiling water for 3 minutes, or according to the packet instructions, until soft. Drain, rinse and drain again, then set aside.

2 Meanwhile, to make the sauce, stir half the water into the arrowroot and set aside. Stir the remaining sauce ingredients and the remaining water together in a small saucepan and bring to the boil. Stir in the arrowroot mixture and continue boiling until the sauce becomes clear, glossy and thick. Remove from the heat and set aside.

3 Heat a wok or large frying pan over a high heat. Add the oil and heat it until it shimmers. Add the onion and stir-fry for 1 minute. Stir in the chicken, carrot and pepper and continue stir-frying for about 3 minutes, or until the chicken is cooked through. Add the bamboo shoots and cashew nuts and stir them around to brown the nuts lightly. Stir the sauce into the wok and heat until it starts to bubble. Add the noodles and use 2 forks to mix them with the chicken and vegetables.

chicken &
green vegetables

ingredients

SERVES 4

250 g/9 oz dried medium
Chinese egg noodles

2 tbsp peanut or corn oil

1 large garlic clove, crushed

1 fresh green chilli, deseeded
and sliced

1 tbsp Chinese five-spice
powder

2 skinless, boneless chicken
breasts, cut into thin strips

2 green peppers, cored,
deseeded and sliced

115 g/4 oz head of broccoli,
cut into small florets

55 g/2 oz green beans,
trimmed and cut into
4-cm/1 1/2-inch pieces

5 tbsp vegetable or chicken
stock

2 tbsp bottled oyster sauce

2 tbsp soy sauce

1 tbsp rice wine or dry sherry

100 g/3 1/2 oz beansprouts

method

1 Cook the noodles in a saucepan of boiling
water for 4 minutes, or according to the
packet instructions, until soft. Drain, rinse
and drain again, then set aside.

2 Heat a wok or large frying pan over a high
heat. Add 1 tablespoon of the oil and heat
until it shimmers. Add the garlic, chilli and
five-spice powder and stir-fry for about
30 seconds. Add the chicken and stir-fry
for 3 minutes, or until it is cooked through.
Use a slotted spoon to remove the chicken
from the wok and set aside.

3 Add the remaining oil to the wok and heat
until it shimmers. Add the peppers, broccoli
and beans and stir-fry for about 2 minutes.
Stir in the stock, oyster sauce, soy sauce and
rice wine and return the chicken to the wok.
Continue stir-frying for about 1 minute, until
the chicken is reheated and the vegetables
are tender but still firm to the bite. Add the
noodles and beansprouts and use 2 forks to
mix all the ingredients together.

chicken chow mein

ingredients

SERVES 4

250 g/9 oz dried medium
    Chinese egg noodles
2 tbsp sunflower oil
280 g/10 oz cooked chicken
    breasts, shredded
1 garlic clove, finely chopped
1 red pepper, deseeded and
    thinly sliced
100 g/3^1/$_2$ oz shiitake
    mushrooms, sliced
6 spring onions, sliced
100 g/3^1/$_2$ oz beansprouts
3 tbsp soy sauce
1 tbsp sesame oil

method

1 Place the noodles in a large bowl or dish and break them up slightly. Pour enough boiling water over the noodles to cover and set aside while preparing the other ingredients.

2 Preheat a wok over a medium heat. Add the sunflower oil and swirl it around to coat the sides of the wok. When the oil is hot, add the shredded chicken, garlic, pepper, mushrooms, spring onions and beansprouts to the wok and stir-fry for about 5 minutes.

3 Drain the noodles thoroughly then add them to the wok, toss well and stir-fry for a further 5 minutes. Drizzle over the soy sauce and sesame oil and toss until thoroughly combined.

4 Transfer to warmed serving bowls and serve immediately.

chicken chow mein baskets

ingredients

SERVES 4

250 g/9 oz fresh thin or
   medium Chinese egg
   noodles

3 tbsp peanut or corn oil, plus
   extra for deep-frying

6 tbsp water

3 tbsp soy sauce

1 tbsp cornflour

4 boneless chicken thighs,
   skinned and chopped

2.5-cm/1-inch piece fresh
   ginger, peeled and finely
   chopped

2 large garlic cloves, crushed

2 celery sticks, thinly sliced

100 g/3^1/2 oz white
   mushrooms, wiped and
   thinly sliced

method

1 Dip a large wire sieve in oil, then line it completely and evenly with one quarter of the tangled noodles. Dip a smaller wire sieve in oil, then position it inside the larger sieve. Heat 10 cm/4 inches of oil in a wok to 180–190°C/350–375°F, or until a cube of bread browns in 30 seconds. Lower the sieves into the oil and deep-fry the noodles for 2–3 minutes, until golden brown. Remove from the oil and drain on kitchen paper. Carefully remove the small sieve and remove the noodle basket. Repeat to make 3 more baskets. Let cool.

2 Stir the water and soy sauce into the cornflour in a small bowl and set aside.

3 Heat a wok or large frying pan over a high heat. Add 2 tablespoons of the oil and heat until it shimmers. Add the chicken and stir-fry for about 3 minutes, or until it is cooked through. Remove the chicken from the wok.

4 Add the remaining oil, then add the ginger, garlic and celery and stir-fry for 2 minutes. Add the mushrooms and continue stir-frying for 2 minutes. Remove the vegetables and add them to the chicken.

5 Pour the cornflour mixture into the wok and bring to the boil, stirring until it thickens. Return the chicken and vegetables to the wok and reheat in the sauce. Divide the chicken mixture between the noodle baskets to serve.

chicken-sesame salad

ingredients

SERVES 4

200 g/7 oz dried thick
    Chinese egg noodles

100 g/3¹/₂ oz mangetout

2 celery sticks

4 cooked skinless chicken
    thighs

sesame dressing

3 tbsp dark soy sauce

3 tbsp Chinese sesame paste

¹/₂ tbsp bottled hoisin sauce

¹/₂ tbsp sugar

¹/₂–1 tbsp bottled sweet chilli
    sauce, to taste

1 tsp rice wine

¹/₂ tbsp boiling water

method

1 To make the dressing, whisk the soy sauce, sesame paste, hoisin sauce, sugar, chilli sauce and rice wine together, then whisk in the boiling water and continue whisking until the sugar dissolves. Set aside until the dressing is cool, then cover and chill until required.

2 Meanwhile, cook the noodles in boiling water for 5 minutes, or according to the packet instructions, until soft. Drain, rinse with cold water to stop the cooking and drain again. Set aside.

3 Use a small, sharp knife to slice the mangetout into thin, lengthways strips, and cut the celery into thin strips. Use your hands to pull the chicken into thin shreds. If you aren't serving the salad immediately, cover the chicken and vegetables and chill.

4 When you are ready to serve, put the noodles, mangetout, celery and chicken in a large bowl. Toss together so all the ingredients are mixed and pour the dressing on top.

cross the bridge noodles

ingredients

SERVES 4

300 g/10¹/₂ oz thin Chinese
egg noodles or rice sticks

200 g/7 oz choi sum or
similar green vegetable

2 litres/3¹/₂ pints chicken
stock

1-cm/¹/₂-inch piece fresh
ginger, peeled

1–2 tsp salt

1 tsp sugar

1 boneless, skinless chicken
breast, finely sliced
diagonally

200 g/7 oz white fish fillet,
finely sliced diagonally

1 tbsp light soy sauce

method

1 Cook the noodles according to the directions
on the packet. When cooked, rinse under cold
water and set aside. Blanch the choi sum in a
large saucepan of boiling water for 30 seconds.
Rinse under cold water and set aside.

2 In a large saucepan, bring the chicken stock
to the boil, then add the ginger, 1 teaspoon of
the salt and the sugar and skim the surface.
Add the chicken and cook for about 4 minutes,
then add the fish slices and simmer for a further
4 minutes, or until the fish and chicken are
cooked through.

3 Add the noodles and choi sum with the light
soy sauce and bring back to the boil. Taste
and adjust the seasoning if necessary. Serve
immediately in large individual noodle bowls.

congee with fish fillet

ingredients

SERVES 6-8

225 g/8 oz short-grain rice

3 litres/5¼ pints water

200 g/7 oz firm white fish
    fillet, flaked

2 tsp salt

½ tsp white pepper

175 g/6 oz lettuce, finely
    shredded

2 tbsp finely shredded
    spring onions

2 tbsp finely shredded
    fresh ginger

3 tbsp light soy sauce,
    to serve

method

1 Wash the rice and place in a large saucepan with the water. Cover and cook for about 2 hours, stirring regularly.

2 Add the fish fillet, salt and pepper. Stir well, then return to the boil and cook for a couple more minutes.

3 To serve, divide the lettuce, spring onions and ginger between large individual bowls. Pour the congee on top. Finally, sprinkle each bowl with 1–2 teaspoons of good-quality soy sauce.

seafood chow mein

ingredients

SERVES 4

85 g/3 oz squid, cleaned

3–4 fresh scallops

85 g/3 oz raw prawns, peeled

1/2 egg white, lightly beaten

2 tsp cornflour, mixed to a
   paste with 2½ tsp water

275 g/9¾ oz dried thin
   Chinese egg noodles

5–6 tbsp vegetable oil

2 tbsp light soy sauce

55 g/2 oz mangetout

1/2 tsp salt

1/2 tsp sugar

1 tsp Chinese rice wine

2 spring onions, shredded
   finely

a few drops of sesame oil

method

1 Open up the squid and score the inside in a criss-cross pattern, then cut into pieces about 2.5 cm/1 inch square. Soak the squid in a bowl of boiling water until all the pieces curl up. Rinse in cold water and drain.

2 Cut each scallop into 3–4 slices. Cut the prawns in half lengthways if large. Mix the scallops and prawns with the egg white and cornflour paste.

3 Cook the noodles in boiling water according to the packet instructions, then drain and rinse under cold water. Drain well, then toss with about 1 tablespoon of the oil.

4 Heat 3 tablespoons of the oil in a preheated wok. Add the noodles and 1 tablespoon of the soy sauce and stir-fry for 2–3 minutes. Remove to a large serving dish.

5 Heat the remaining oil in the wok and add the mangetout and seafood. Stir-fry for about 2 minutes, then add the salt, sugar, rice wine, remaining soy sauce and about half the spring onions. Blend well and add a little water if necessary. Pour the seafood mixture on top of the noodles and sprinkle with sesame oil. Garnish with the remaining spring onions and serve immediately.

crab fried rice

ingredients

SERVES 4

150 g/5 1/2 oz long-grain rice

2 tbsp peanut oil

125 g/4 1/2 oz canned white
    crabmeat, drained

1 leek, sliced

150 g/5 1/2 oz beansprouts

2 eggs, beaten

1 tbsp light soy sauce

2 tsp lime juice

1 tsp sesame oil

salt

sliced lime, to garnish

method

1 Cook the rice in a saucepan of lightly salted boiling water for 15 minutes. Drain, rinse under cold running water and drain again.

2 Heat the oil in a preheated wok or large, heavy-based frying pan until it is really hot. Add the crabmeat, leek and beansprouts to the wok or frying pan and stir-fry for 2–3 minutes. Remove the mixture with a slotted spoon and reserve.

3 Add the eggs to the wok and cook, stirring occasionally, for 2–3 minutes, until they begin to set. Stir the rice and the crabmeat mixture into the eggs.

4 Add the soy sauce and lime juice to the mixture in the wok. Cook for 1 minute, stirring to combine. Sprinkle with the sesame oil and toss lightly to mix.

5 Transfer the crab fried rice to a serving dish, garnish with the sliced lime and serve immediately.

chinese prawn salad

ingredients

SERVES 4

250 g/9 oz dried thin Chinese
    egg noodles

3 tbsp sunflower oil

1 tbsp sesame oil

1 tbsp sesame seeds

175 g/6 oz beansprouts

1 mango, peeled, pitted
    and sliced

6 spring onions, sliced

75 g/2¾ oz radishes, sliced

350 g/12 oz cooked peeled
    prawns

2 tbsp light soy sauce

1 tbsp sherry

method

1 Put the noodles in a large, heatproof bowl and pour over enough boiling water to cover. Set aside for 10 minutes, then drain thoroughly and pat dry with kitchen paper.

2 Heat the sunflower oil in a large, preheated wok. Add the noodles and stir-fry for 5 minutes, tossing frequently.

3 Remove the wok from the heat and add the sesame oil, sesame seeds and beansprouts, tossing to mix well.

4 Mix the mango, spring onions, radishes, prawns, soy sauce and sherry together in a separate bowl. Toss the prawn mixture with the noodles. Alternatively, arrange the noodles around the edge of a serving plate and pile the prawn mixture into the centre. Serve immediately.

egg fu yung

ingredients

SERVES 4–6

2 eggs

1/2 tsp salt

pinch of white pepper

1 tsp melted butter

2 tbsp vegetable or peanut oil

1 tsp finely chopped garlic

1 small onion, finely sliced

1 green pepper, finely sliced

450 g/1 lb cooked rice,
    chilled

1 tbsp light soy sauce

1 tbsp finely chopped
    spring onions

150 g/5 oz beansprouts,
    trimmed

2 drops of sesame oil

method

1 Beat the eggs with the salt and pepper. Heat the butter in a frying pan and pour in the eggs. Cook as an omelette, until set, then remove from the pan and cut into slivers.

2 In a preheated wok or deep saucepan, heat the oil and stir-fry the garlic until fragrant. Add the onion and stir-fry for 1 minute, then add the green pepper and stir-fry for a further 1 minute. Stir in the rice and, when the grains are separated, stir in the light soy sauce and cook for 1 minute.

3 Add the spring onions and egg strips and stir well, then finally add the beansprouts and sesame oil. Stir-fry for 1 minute and serve.

szechuan noodles

ingredients

SERVES 4

1 large carrot

250 g/9 oz dried thick
   Chinese egg noodles

2 tbsp peanut or corn oil

2 large garlic cloves, very
   finely chopped

1 large red onion, cut in half
   and thinly sliced

125 ml/4 fl oz vegetable stock
   or water

2 tbsp bottled chilli bean sauce

2 tbsp Chinese sesame paste

1 tbsp dried Szechuan
   peppercorns, roasted
   and ground

1 tsp light soy sauce

2 small pak choi or other
   Chinese cabbage, cut
   into quarters

method

1 Peel the carrot and cut off both ends, then grate it lengthways on the coarsest side of a grater to make long, thin strips. Set the carrot strips aside.

2 Cook the noodles in a saucepan of boiling water for 4 minutes, or according to the packet instructions, until soft. Drain and rinse with cold water to stop the cooking, then set aside.

3 Heat a wok or large frying pan over a high heat. Add the oil and heat until it shimmers. Add the garlic and onion and stir-fry for 1 minute. Add the vegetable stock, chilli bean sauce, sesame paste, ground Szechuan peppercorns and soy sauce and bring to the boil, stirring to blend the ingredients together. Add the pak choi quarters and carrot strips and continue stir-frying for 1–2 minutes, until they are just wilted. Add the noodles and continue stir-frying, using 2 forks to mix all the ingredients together. Serve the noodles when they are hot.

hot-&-sour noodle salad

ingredients

SERVES 4

350 g/12 oz dried rice
 vermicelli noodles

4 tbsp sesame oil

3 tbsp soy sauce

juice of 2 limes

1 tsp sugar

4 spring onions, finely sliced

1–2 tsp hot chilli sauce

2 tbsp chopped fresh
 coriander

method

1 Prepare the noodles according to the packet instructions. Drain, put in a bowl and toss with half the oil.

2 Mix the remaining oil, soy sauce, lime juice, sugar, spring onions and chilli sauce together in a bowl. Stir into the noodles.

3 Stir in the coriander and serve.

sweet-&-sour vegetables on noodle pancakes

ingredients

SERVES 4

115 g/4 oz dried thin
    cellophane noodles

6 eggs

4 spring onions, sliced
    diagonally

$2^1/_2$ tbsp peanut or corn oil

900 g/2 lb selection of
    vegetables, such as carrots,
    baby corn, cauliflower,
    broccoli, mangetout,
    mushrooms and onions,
    peeled as necessary and
    chopped into same-sized
    pieces

100 g/$3^1/_2$ oz canned bamboo
    shoots, drained

200 g/7 oz bottled sweet-and-
    sour sauce

salt and pepper

method

1 Soak the noodles in enough lukewarm water to cover and set aside for 20 minutes, or according to the packet instructions, until soft. Drain them well and use scissors to cut into 7.5-cm/3-inch pieces.

2 Beat the eggs, then stir in the noodles, spring onions, salt and pepper. Heat a 20-cm/8-inch frying pan over a high heat. Add 1 tablespoon of oil and swirl it around. Pour in a quarter of the egg mixture and tilt the frying pan so it covers the bottom. Lower the heat to medium and cook for 1 minute, or until the thin pancake is set. Flip it over and add a little extra oil, if necessary. Continue cooking until beginning to colour. Transfer to a plate and keep warm in a low oven while you make 3 more pancakes.

3 After you've made 4 pancakes, heat a wok or large, heavy-based frying pan over a high heat. Add $1^1/_2$ tablespoons of oil and heat until it shimmers. Add the thickest vegetables, such as carrots, first and stir-fry for 30 seconds. Gradually add the remaining vegetables and bamboo shoots. Stir in the sauce and stir-fry until all the vegetables are tender and the sauce is hot. Spoon the vegetables and sauce over the pancakes.

egg-fried rice with peas

ingredients

SERVES 4

150 g/5^1/$_2$ oz long-grain rice

3 eggs, beaten

2 tbsp vegetable oil

2 garlic cloves, crushed

4 spring onions, chopped

125 g/4^1/$_2$ oz cooked peas

1 tbsp light soy sauce

pinch of salt

shredded spring onions,
    to garnish

method

1 Cook the rice in a saucepan of boiling water for 10–12 minutes until almost cooked, but not soft. Drain well, rinse under cold running water and drain thoroughly.

2 Place the beaten eggs in a saucepan and cook over a low heat, stirring constantly, until softly scrambled. Remove the pan from the heat and set aside.

3 Preheat a wok over a medium heat. Add the oil and swirl it around to coat the sides of the wok. When the oil is hot, add the garlic, spring onions and peas and sauté, stirring occasionally, for 1–2 minutes.

4 Stir the rice into the mixture in the wok, mixing to combine. Add the eggs, soy sauce and salt to the wok and stir to mix in the eggs thoroughly.

5 Transfer to serving dishes and serve garnished with the shredded spring onions.

spicy tofu

ingredients

SERVES 4

250 g/9 oz firm tofu, rinsed
   and drained thoroughly
   and cut into 1-cm/$^1/_2$-inch
   cubes

4 tbsp peanut oil

1 tbsp grated fresh ginger

3 garlic cloves, crushed

4 spring onions, thinly sliced

1 head of broccoli, cut into
   florets

1 carrot, cut into batons

1 yellow pepper, thinly sliced

250 g/9 oz shiitake
   mushrooms, thinly sliced

steamed rice, to serve (see
   page 216)

marinade

5 tbsp vegetable stock

2 tsp cornflour

2 tbsp soy sauce

1 tbsp caster sugar

pinch of chilli flakes

method

1 Combine all the ingredients for the marinade in a large bowl. Add the tofu and toss well to cover in the marinade. Set aside to marinate for 20 minutes.

2 In a large frying pan or wok, heat 2 tablespoons of the peanut oil and stir-fry the tofu with its marinade until brown and crispy. Remove from the frying pan and set aside.

3 Heat the remaining 2 tablespoons of peanut oil in the frying pan and stir-fry the ginger, garlic and spring onions for 30 seconds. Add the broccoli, carrot, yellow pepper and mushrooms to the frying pan and cook for 5–6 minutes. Return the tofu to the frying pan and stir-fry to reheat. Serve immediately over steamed rice.

a firepot of mushrooms & tofu

ingredients

SERVES 4

55 g/2 oz dried Chinese
    mushrooms

115 g/4 oz firm tofu, drained

2 tbsp bottled sweet chilli
    sauce

2 tbsp peanut or corn oil

2 large garlic cloves, chopped

1-cm/^{1}/$_2$-inch piece fresh
    ginger, peeled and finely
    chopped

1 red onion, sliced

^{1}/$_2$ tbsp Szechuan peppercorns,
    lightly crushed

55 g/2 oz canned straw
    mushrooms, drained
    weight, rinsed

vegetable stock or water

1 star anise

pinch of sugar

soy sauce, to taste

115 g/4 oz dried thin
    cellophane noodles

method

1 Soak the mushrooms in enough boiling water to cover for 20 minutes, or until soft. Cut the tofu into bite-sized chunks, coat with the chilli sauce and marinate.

2 Just before you are ready to start cooking, strain the soaked mushrooms through a sieve lined with kitchen paper, reserving the soaking liquid. Heat the oil in a medium-size ovenproof casserole or large frying pan with a lid. Add the garlic and ginger and stir them around for 30 seconds. Add the onion and peppercorns and keep stirring until the onion is almost tender. Add the tofu, the soaked mushrooms and the canned mushrooms and stir carefully so the tofu doesn't break up.

3 Add the reserved mushroom soaking liquid to the wok with just enough vegetable stock to cover. Stir in the star anise, a pinch of sugar and several dashes of soy sauce. Bring to the boil, then reduce the heat, cover and simmer for 5 minutes. Add the noodles, re-cover and simmer for a further 5 minutes, or until the noodles are tender. The noodles should be covered with liquid, so add extra stock at this point, if necessary. Use a fork or wooden spoon to stir the noodles into the other ingredients. Add more soy sauce, if liked.

vegetables &
side dishes

Even if you aren't cooking a full Chinese meal, it's worth cooking your vegetables Chinese-style – they are nutritious and absolutely bursting with flavour, colour and interest. The wok is used to great effect here, too, and vegetables cook so rapidly that they retain their texture to perfection. If you don't have a wok, a deep saucepan or heavy-based frying pan can be used instead. Another item of equipment you might consider is a little 'claypot' with a lid and a glazed inside, which is excellent for braising – Braised Straw Mushrooms simply melt in the mouth.

Not all vegetable dishes are vegetarian – for example, Chunky Potatoes with Coriander Leaves includes a little pork, and it is not unusual to use chicken stock in the cooking or to add oyster sauce for flavour. If you are looking for a vegetarian main dish, Sweet-&-Sour Vegetables with Cashew Nuts and Vegetable & Coconut Curry are delicious options.

The Chinese are very good at eating their greens – and very cook at cooking them, too. Stir-fried French Beans with Red Pepper, Broccoli & Mangetout Stir-fry, Stir-fried Chinese Greens and Garlic Spinach Stir-fry are irresistibly tempting and will convert anyone who was ever put off by overcooked vegetables!

chinese tomato salad

ingredients

SERVES 4–6

2 large tomatoes

dressing

1 tbsp finely chopped
    spring onions

1 tsp finely chopped garlic

$1/2$ tsp sesame oil

1 tbsp white rice vinegar

$1/2$ tsp salt

pinch of white pepper

pinch of sugar

method

1 Mix together all the ingredients for the dressing and set aside.

2 Thinly slice the tomatoes. Arrange on a plate and pour the dressing over the top. Serve immediately.

cabbage & cucumber in a vinegar dressing

ingredients

SERVES 4–6

225 g/8 oz Chinese cabbage, very finely shredded

1 tsp salt

1 cucumber, peeled, deseeded and finely chopped into short thin sticks

1 tsp sesame oil

2 tbsp white rice vinegar

1 tsp sugar

method

1 Sprinkle the cabbage with the salt and set aside for at least 10 minutes. Drain the cabbage if necessary, then mix with the cucumber pieces.

2 Whisk together the sesame oil, vinegar and sugar and toss the vegetables in it. Serve immediately.

classic stir-fried vegetables

ingredients

SERVES 4

3 tbsp sesame oil

6 spring onions, finely
    chopped, plus 2 spring
    onions, finely chopped,
    to garnish

1 garlic clove, crushed

1 tbsp grated fresh ginger

1 head of broccoli,
    cut into florets

1 orange or yellow pepper,
    roughly chopped

125 g/4$\frac{1}{2}$ oz red cabbage,
    shredded

125 g/4$\frac{1}{2}$ oz baby corn

175 g/6 oz portobello or large
    cup mushrooms, thinly
    sliced

200 g/7 oz fresh beansprouts

250 g/9 oz canned water
    chestnuts, drained

4 tsp soy sauce; or to taste

cooked wild rice, to serve

method

1 Heat 2 tablespoons of the oil in a large
frying pan or wok over a high heat. Stir-fry
the 6 chopped spring onions with the garlic
and ginger for 30 seconds.

2 Add the broccoli, pepper and red cabbage
and stir-fry for 1–2 minutes. Mix in the baby
corn and mushrooms and stir-fry for a further
1–2 minutes.

3 Finally, add the beansprouts and water
chestnuts and cook for 2 minutes. Pour in
the soy sauce and stir well.

4 Serve immediately over cooked wild rice,
garnished with the remaining spring onions.

sweet-&-sour vegetables with cashew nuts

ingredients

SERVES 4

1 tbsp vegetable or peanut oil

1 tsp chilli oil

2 onions, sliced

2 carrots, thinly sliced

2 courgettes, thinly sliced

115 g/4 oz head of broccoli, cut into florets

115 g/4 oz white mushrooms, sliced

115 g/4 oz small pak choi, halved

2 tbsp brown sugar

2 tbsp Thai soy sauce

1 tbsp rice vinegar

55 g/2 oz cashew nuts

method

1 Heat both the oils in a preheated wok or frying pan, add the onions and stir-fry for 1–2 minutes until beginning to soften.

2 Add the carrots, courgettes and broccoli and stir-fry for 2–3 minutes. Add the mushrooms, pak choi, sugar, soy sauce and vinegar and stir-fry for 1–2 minutes.

3 Meanwhile, heat a dry, heavy-based frying pan over a high heat, add the cashew nuts and cook, shaking the frying pan frequently, until lightly toasted. Sprinkle the cashew nuts over the stir-fry and serve immediately.

vegetable & coconut curry

ingredients

SERVES 4

1 onion, roughly chopped

3 garlic cloves, thinly sliced

2.5-cm/1-inch piece fresh
ginger, thinly sliced

2 fresh green chillies,
deseeded and finely
chopped

1 tbsp vegetable oil

1 tsp ground turmeric

1 tsp ground coriander

1 tsp ground cumin

1 kg/2 lb 4 oz mixed
vegetables, such as
cauliflower, courgettes,
potatoes, carrots and
green beans, cut into
chunks

200 g/7 oz coconut cream or
coconut milk

salt and pepper

2 tbsp chopped fresh
coriander, to garnish

freshly cooked rice, to serve

method

1 Put the onion, garlic, ginger and chillies in a
food processor and process until almost smooth.

2 Heat the oil in a large, heavy-based saucepan
over a medium–low heat, add the onion mixture
and cook, stirring constantly, for 5 minutes.

3 Add the turmeric, coriander and cumin and
cook, stirring frequently, for 3–4 minutes.
Add the vegetables and stir to coat in the
spice paste.

4 Add the coconut cream to the vegetables,
cover and simmer for 30–40 minutes until the
vegetables are tender.

5 Season with salt and pepper, garnish with
the chopped fresh coriander and serve with
freshly cooked rice.

stir-fried french beans with red pepper

ingredients

SERVES 4–6

280 g/10 oz French beans,
    cut into 6-cm/2^{1}/$_{2}$-inch
    lengths

1 tbsp vegetable or peanut oil

1 red pepper, slivered

pinch of salt

pinch of sugar

method

1 Blanch the beans in a large saucepan of boiling water for 30 seconds. Drain and set aside.

2 In a preheated wok or deep saucepan, heat the oil and stir-fry the beans for 1 minute over a high heat. Add the pepper and stir-fry for a further 1 minute. Sprinkle the salt and sugar on top and serve.

spicy french beans

ingredients

SERVES 4

200 g/7 oz French beans,
    trimmed and cut
    diagonally into 3–4 pieces
2 tbsp vegetable or peanut oil
4 dried chillies, cut into
    2 or 3 pieces
1/2 tsp Szechuan peppers
1 garlic clove, finely sliced
6 thin slices of fresh ginger
2 spring onions, white part
    only, cut diagonally into
    thin pieces
pinch of sea salt

method

1 Blanch the beans in a large saucepan of boiling water for 30 seconds. Drain and set aside.

2 In a preheated wok or deep saucepan, heat 1 tablespoon of the oil. Over a low heat, stir-fry the beans for about 5 minutes, or until they are beginning to wrinkle. Remove from the wok and set aside.

3 Add the remaining oil and stir-fry the chillies and peppers until they are fragrant. Add the garlic, ginger and spring onions and stir-fry until they begin to soften. Throw in the beans and toss, then add the sea salt and serve immediately.

stir-fried broccoli

ingredients

SERVES 4

2 tbsp vegetable oil

2 medium heads of broccoli,
  cut into florets

2 tbsp soy sauce

1 tsp cornflour

1 tbsp caster sugar

1 tsp grated fresh ginger

1 garlic clove, crushed

pinch of hot chilli flakes

1 tsp toasted sesame seeds,
  to garnish

method

1 In a large frying pan or wok, heat the oil until almost smoking. Stir-fry the broccoli for 4–5 minutes.

2 In a small bowl, combine the soy sauce, cornflour, sugar, ginger, garlic and hot chilli flakes. Add the mixture to the broccoli. Cook over gentle heat, stirring constantly, for 2–3 minutes until the sauce thickens slightly.

3 Transfer to a serving dish, garnish with the sesame seeds and serve immediately.

broccoli & mangetout stir-fry

ingredients

SERVES 4

2 tbsp vegetable or peanut oil

dash of sesame oil

1 garlic clove, finely chopped

225 g/8 oz head of broccoli,
    cut into small florets

115 g/4 oz mangetout,
    trimmed

225 g/8 oz Chinese cabbage,
    chopped into 1-cm/
    1/2-inch slices

5–6 spring onions, finely
    chopped

1/2 tsp salt

2 tbsp light soy sauce

1 tbsp Shaoxing rice wine

1 tsp toasted sesame seeds,
    to garnish

method

1 In a preheated wok or deep saucepan, heat the oils, then add the garlic and stir-fry vigorously. Add all the vegetables and salt and stir-fry over a high heat, tossing rapidly, for about 3 minutes.

2 Pour in the light soy sauce and Shaoxing and cook for a further 2 minutes.

3 Transfer to a serving dish, garnish with the sesame seeds and serve hot.

choi sum in oyster sauce

ingredients

SERVES 4–6

300 g/10¹/₂ oz choi sum

1 tbsp vegetable or peanut oil

1 tsp finely chopped garlic

1 tbsp oyster sauce

method

1 Blanch the choi sum in a large saucepan of boiling water for 30 seconds. Drain and set aside.

2 In a preheated wok or deep saucepan, heat the oil and stir-fry the garlic until fragrant. Add the choi sum and toss for 1 minute. Stir in the oyster sauce and serve.

stir-fried chinese greens

ingredients

SERVES 4

1 tbsp vegetable or peanut oil

1 tsp finely chopped garlic

225 g/8 oz leafy Chinese
    greens, roughly chopped

1/2 tsp salt

method

1 In a preheated wok or deep saucepan, heat the oil and stir-fry the garlic until fragrant.

2 Over a high heat, toss in the Chinese greens and salt and stir-fry for 1 minute maximum. Serve immediately.

hot-&-sour cabbage

ingredients

SERVES 4

450 g/1 lb firm white cabbage

1 tbsp vegetable or peanut oil

10 Szechuan peppers or
    more, to taste

3 dried chillies, roughly
    chopped

$1/2$ tsp salt

1 tsp white rice vinegar

dash of sesame oil

pinch of sugar

method

1 To prepare the cabbage, discard the outer leaves and tough stems. Chop the cabbage into 3-cm/1 1/4-inch squares, breaking up the chunks. Rinse thoroughly in cold water.

2 In a preheated wok or deep saucepan, heat the oil and cook the peppers until fragrant. Stir in the chillies. Throw in the cabbage, a little at a time, together with the salt, and stir-fry for 2 minutes.

3 Add the vinegar, sesame oil and sugar and cook for a further minute, or until the cabbage is tender. Serve immediately.

garlic spinach stir-fry

ingredients

SERVES 4

6 tbsp vegetable oil

6 garlic cloves, crushed

2 tbsp black bean sauce

3 tomatoes, roughly chopped

900 g/2 lb spinach, tough
    stalks removed, roughly
    chopped

1 tsp chilli sauce, or to taste

2 tbsp fresh lemon juice

salt and pepper

method

1 Heat the oil in a preheated wok or large frying pan over a high heat, add the garlic, black bean sauce and tomatoes and stir-fry for 1 minute.

2 Stir in the spinach, chilli sauce and lemon juice and mix well. Cook, stirring frequently, for 3 minutes, or until the spinach is just wilted. Season with salt and pepper. Remove from the heat and serve immediately.

chunky potatoes with coriander leaves

ingredients

SERVES 6–8

4 potatoes, peeled and cut
  into large chunks

vegetable or peanut oil,
  for frying

100 g/3^1/$_2$ oz pork, not too
  lean, finely chopped or
  minced

1 green pepper, finely
  chopped

1 tbsp finely chopped spring
  onions, white part only

2 tsp salt

^{1}/$_2$ tsp white pepper

pinch of sugar

2–3 tbsp cooking water from
  the potatoes

2 tbsp chopped coriander
  leaves

method

1 Boil the potatoes in a large saucepan of boiling water for 15–25 minutes, or until cooked. Drain, reserving some of the water.

2 In a wok or deep saucepan, heat plenty of the oil and cook the potatoes until golden. Drain and set aside.

3 In the clean preheated wok or saucepan, heat 1 tablespoon of the oil and stir-fry the pork, pepper and spring onions for 1 minute. Season with the salt, pepper and sugar and stir-fry for a further 1 minute.

4 Stir in the potato chunks and add the water. Cook for 2–3 minutes, or until the potatoes are warmed through. Turn off the heat, then stir in the coriander and serve warm.

szechuan fried aubergine

ingredients

SERVES 4

vegetable or peanut oil,
    for frying
4 aubergines, halved
    lengthways and cut
    diagonally into 5-cm/
    2-inch pieces
1 tbsp chilli bean sauce
2 tsp finely chopped
    fresh ginger
2 tsp finely chopped garlic
2–3 tbsp chicken stock
1 tsp sugar
1 tsp light soy sauce
3 spring onions, finely
    chopped

method

1 In a preheated wok or deep pan, heat the oil and cook the aubergine pieces for 3–4 minutes, or until lightly browned. Drain on kitchen paper and set aside.

2 In the clean wok or deep saucepan, heat 2 tablespoons of the oil. Add the chilli bean sauce and stir-fry rapidly, then add the ginger and garlic and stir until fragrant. Add the stock, sugar and light soy sauce. Toss in the fried aubergine pieces and simmer for 2 minutes. Stir in the spring onions and serve.

aubergine with red peppers

ingredients

SERVES 4

3 tbsp vegetable or peanut oil

1 garlic clove, finely chopped

3 aubergines, halved
   lengthways and cut
   diagonally into 2.5-cm/
   1-inch pieces

1 tsp white rice vinegar

1 red pepper, finely sliced

2 tbsp light soy sauce

1 tsp sugar

1 tbsp finely chopped
   coriander leaves, to
   garnish

method

1 In a preheated wok or deep saucepan, heat the oil. When it begins to smoke, toss in the garlic and stir-fry until fragrant, then add the aubergine. Stir-fry for 30 seconds, then add the vinegar. Turn down the heat and cook, covered, for 5 minutes, stirring occasionally.

2 When the aubergine pieces are soft, add the pepper and stir. Add the light soy sauce and sugar and cook, uncovered, for 2 minutes.

3 Turn off the heat and rest for 2 minutes. Transfer to a dish, then garnish with coriander and serve.

oyster mushrooms & vegetables with peanut chilli sauce

ingredients

SERVES 4

1 tbsp sesame oil

4 spring onions, sliced finely

1 carrot, cut into batons

1 courgette, cut into batons

1/2 head of broccoli,
    cut into florets

450 g/1 lb oyster mushrooms,
    thinly sliced

2 tbsp crunchy peanut butter

1 tsp chilli powder, or to taste

3 tbsp water

cooked rice or noodles,
    to serve

wedges of lime, to garnish

method

1 Heat the oil in a frying pan or wok until almost smoking. Stir-fry the spring onions for 1 minute. Add the carrot and courgette and stir-fry for a further 1 minute. Then add the broccoli and cook for 1 minute more.

2 Stir in the mushrooms and cook until they are soft and at least half the liquid they produce has evaporated. Add the peanut butter and stir well. Season with the chilli powder. Finally, add the water and cook for a further 1 minute.

3 Serve over rice or noodles and garnish with wedges of lime.

braised straw mushrooms

ingredients

SERVES 4

1 tbsp vegetable or peanut oil

1 tsp finely chopped garlic

175 g/6 oz straw mushrooms,
  washed but left whole

2 tsp fermented black beans,
  rinsed and lightly mashed

1 tsp sugar

1 tbsp light soy sauce

1 tsp dark soy sauce

method

1 Heat the oil in a small claypot or saucepan. Cook the garlic until fragrant, then add the mushrooms and stir well to coat in the oil.

2 Add the beans, sugar and soy sauces, then lower the heat and simmer, covered, for about 10 minutes, or until the mushrooms are soft.

bamboo shoots with tofu

ingredients

SERVES 4–6

3 dried Chinese mushrooms,
    soaked in warm water for
    20 minutes

55 g/2 oz baby pak choi

vegetable or peanut oil, for
    deep-frying

450 g/1 lb firm tofu, cut into
    2.5-cm/1-inch squares

55 g/2 oz fresh or canned
    bamboo shoots, rinsed
    and finely sliced (if using
    fresh shoots, boil in water
    first for 30 minutes)

1 tsp oyster sauce

1 tsp light soy sauce

method

1 Squeeze out any excess water from the mushrooms and finely slice, discarding any tough stems. Blanch the pak choi in a large saucepan of boiling water for 30 seconds. Drain and set aside.

2 Heat enough oil for deep-frying in a wok, deep-fat fryer, or large heavy-based saucepan until it reaches 180–190°C/350–375°F, or until a cube of bread browns in 30 seconds. Cook the tofu cubes until golden brown. Remove, then drain and set aside.

3 In a preheated wok or deep saucepan, heat 1 tablespoon of the oil, then toss in the mushrooms and pak choi and stir. Add the tofu and bamboo shoots with the oyster and soy sauces. Heat through and serve.

stir-fried beansprouts

ingredients

SERVES 4

1 tbsp vegetable or peanut oil

225 g/8 oz beansprouts,
    trimmed

2 tbsp finely chopped
    spring onions

$1/2$ tsp salt

pinch of sugar

method

1 In a preheated wok or deep saucepan, heat the oil and stir-fry the beansprouts with the spring onions for about 1 minute. Add the salt and sugar and stir.

2 Remove from the heat and serve immediately.

egg-fried rice

ingredients

SERVES 4

2 tbsp vegetable or peanut oil

12 oz/350 g cooked rice, chilled

1 egg, well beaten

method

1 Heat the oil in a preheated wok or deep saucepan and stir-fry the rice for 1 minute, breaking it down as much as possible into individual grains.

2 Quickly add the egg, stirring, so as to coat each piece of rice. Stir until the egg is cooked and the rice, as far as possible, is in single grains. Serve immediately.

steamed white rice

ingredients

SERVES 3–4

225 g/8 oz rice

cold water

method

1 Wash the rice. Place in a saucepan with the same volume of water plus a little extra (the water should just cover the rice). Bring to the boil, then cover and simmer for about 15 minutes.

2 Turn off the heat and let the rice continue to cook in its own steam for about 5 minutes. At this point, the grains should be cooked through but not sticking together.

desserts

If the highlight of your visit to your favourite Chinese restaurant is the moment when the waiter sets down a plate of Banana Fritters or Toffee Apple Slices in front of you, then this chapter will really appeal to you!

In authentic Chinese cuisine, the sweet things that are known as 'desserts' in the Western world are either eaten separately from a meal, or are served as part of the meal whenever they happen to be ready. They are also eaten as snacks at any time of the day. Baked sweet treats, such as Almond Cookies, have only recently been added to the repertoire, there being no oven in a traditional Chinese kitchen. Seasonal fruit, perhaps with a little sugar added, is the most popular dessert in China – Fresh Fruit Salad with Lemon Juice is a simple but refreshing dish, and looks very attractive made with different varieties of melon. For a more sophisticated fruit-based recipe, Mango Pudding blends East with West with great success.

Chinese rice puddings are made with glutinous rice, which is soaked in cold water for at least 2 hours before it is cooked. For an impressive end to a festive Chinese meal, Eight-treasures Sweet Rice Cake, layered with dried fruits and sweet red bean paste, will please your palate and also bring you luck!

pears in honey syrup

ingredients

SERVES 4

4 medium-ripe pears

200 ml/7 fl oz water

1 tsp sugar

1 tbsp honey

method

1 Peel each pear, leaving the stem intact. Wrap each one in aluminium foil and place in a saucepan with the stems resting on the side of the pan. Add enough water to cover at least half of the height of the pears. Bring to the boil and simmer for 30 minutes. Remove the pears and carefully remove the foil, reserving any juices. Set the pears aside to cool.

2 Bring the measured water to the boil. Add any pear juices, the sugar and the honey and boil for 5 minutes. Remove from the heat and let cool a little.

3 To serve, place each pear in a small individual dish. Pour over a little syrup and serve just warm.

fresh fruit salad with lemon juice

ingredients

SERVES 4–6

2 tbsp sugar

450 g/1 lb mixed melons,
cut into balls or cubes

2 bananas, thinly sliced
diagonally

juice of 1 lemon

method

1 In a large bowl, sprinkle the sugar over the melon pieces.

2 Toss the banana in the lemon juice and add to the melon, then serve immediately.

mango pudding

ingredients

SERVES 6

25 g/1 oz sago, soaked in water
    for at least 20 minutes

250 ml/9 fl oz warm water

2 tablespoons sugar

1 large ripe mango, weighing
    about 280 g/10 oz

200 ml/7 fl oz whipping
    cream

1 tbsp powdered gelatine,
    dissolved in 250 ml/
    9 fl oz warm water

method

1 Put the drained sago and warm water in a saucepan. Bring to the boil, then cook over a low heat for 10 minutes, stirring frequently, until thick. Stir in the sugar and let cool.

2 Peel the mango and slice off the flesh from the stone. Reduce the mango to a smooth paste in a food processor or blender. Stir in the cream and then the gelatine.

3 Combine all the ingredients. Pour into 6 small bowls and chill in the refrigerator until set.

toffee bananas

ingredients

SERVES 4

70 g/2¹/₂ oz self-raising flour

1 egg, beaten

5 tbsp iced water

4 large, ripe bananas

3 tbsp lemon juice

2 tbsp rice flour

vegetable oil, for deep-frying

caramel

115 g/4 oz caster sugar

4 tbsp iced water, plus an
    extra bowl of iced water
    for setting

2 tbsp sesame seeds

method

1 Sift the flour into a bowl. Make a well in the centre, add the egg and iced water and beat from the centre outwards, until combined into a smooth batter.

2 Peel the bananas and cut into 5-cm/2-inch pieces. Gently shape them into balls with your hands. Brush with lemon juice to prevent discoloration, then roll them in rice flour until coated.

3 Pour oil into a saucepan to a depth of 6 cm/ 2¹/₂ inches and preheat to 180–190°C/350– 375°F, or until a cube of bread browns in 30 seconds. Coat the balls in the batter and cook in batches in the hot oil for about 2 minutes each, until golden. Lift them out and drain on kitchen paper.

4 To make the caramel, put the sugar into a small saucepan over a low heat. Add 4 tablespoons of iced water and heat, stirring, until the sugar dissolves. Simmer for 5 minutes, remove from the heat and stir in the sesame seeds. Toss the banana balls in the caramel, scoop them out and drop into the bowl of iced water to set. Lift them out and divide between individual serving bowls. Serve hot.

banana fritters

ingredients

SERVES 4

70 g/2¹/₂ oz plain flour
2 tbsp rice flour
1 tbsp caster sugar
1 egg, separated
150 ml/5 fl oz coconut milk
4 large bananas
sunflower oil for deep-frying
1 tsp icing sugar
1 tsp ground cinnamon
lime wedges, to decorate

method

1 Sift the plain flour, rice flour and sugar into a bowl and make a well in the centre. Add the egg yolk and coconut milk. Beat the mixture until a smooth, thick batter forms.

2 Whisk the egg white in a clean, dry bowl until stiff enough to hold soft peaks. Fold it into the batter lightly and evenly.

3 Heat a 6-cm/2¹/₂-inch depth of oil in a large saucepan to 180–190°C/350–375°F, or until a cube of bread browns in 30 seconds. Cut the bananas in half crossways, then dip them quickly into the batter to coat them.

4 Drop the bananas carefully into the hot oil and deep-fry in batches for 2–3 minutes until golden brown, turning once.

5 Drain on kitchen paper. Sprinkle with icing sugar and cinnamon and serve immediately, with lime wedges for squeezing juice as desired.

toffee apple slices

ingredients

SERVES 4

4 apples, peeled, cored and
    each cut into thick slices
vegetable or peanut oil, for
    deep-frying

batter
115 g/4 oz plain flour
1 egg, beaten
125 ml/4 fl oz cold water

toffee syrup
4 tbsp sesame oil
225 g/8 oz sugar
2 tbsp sesame seeds, toasted

method

1 To prepare the batter, sift the flour and stir in the egg. Slowly add the water, beating to form a smooth and thick batter. Dip each apple slice in the batter.

2 Heat enough oil for deep-frying in a wok, deep-fat fryer, or large heavy-based saucepan until it reaches 180–190°C/350–375°F, or until a cube of bread browns in 30 seconds. Deep-fry the apple slices until golden brown. Drain and set aside.

3 To make the toffee syrup, heat the sesame oil in a small, heavy-based saucepan and, when beginning to smoke, add the sugar, stirring constantly, until the mixture caramelizes and turns golden. Remove from the heat, then stir in the sesame seeds and pour into a large flat saucepan.

4 Over very low heat, place the apple slices in the syrup, turning once. When coated, dip each slice in cold water. Serve immediately.

almond jelly in ginger sauce

ingredients

SERVES 6–8

jelly

850 ml/1¹/₂ pints water

5 g/¹/₈ oz agar-agar

225 g/8 oz sugar

125 ml/4 fl oz evaporated
milk

1 tsp almond extract

sauce

100 g/3¹/₂ oz piece of fresh
ginger, roughly chopped

850 ml/1¹/₂ pints water

55 g/2 oz brown sugar

method

1 To prepare the jelly, bring the water to the boil. Add the agar-agar and stir until dissolved. Stir in the sugar.

2 Pour through a sieve into a shallow dish. Pour in the evaporated milk, stirring constantly. When slightly cooled, stir in the almond extract, then chill in the refrigerator.

3 To make the ginger sauce, boil the ginger, water and sugar in a covered saucepan for at least 1¹/₂ hours, or until the sauce is golden in colour. Discard the ginger.

4 With a knife, cut thin slices of the jelly and arrange in individual bowls. Pour a little ginger sauce, warm or cold, over the jelly.

eight-treasures sweet rice cake

ingredients

SERVES 6–8

225 g/8 oz glutinous rice,
    soaked in cold water for at
    least 2 hours

100 g/3^1/$_2$ oz sugar

2 tablespoons vegetable fat

2 dried kumquats, finely
    chopped

3 prunes, finely chopped

5 dried red dates, soaked for
    20 minutes in warm water,
    then finely chopped

1 tsp raisins

12 lotus seeds (if using dried
    seeds, soak in warm water
    for at least 1 hour)

100 g/3^1/$_2$ oz sweet red bean
    paste

method

1 Steam the glutinous rice for about 20 minutes,
or until soft. Set aside. When the rice is cool,
mix in the sugar and vegetable fat by hand to
form a sticky mass.

2 Arrange the dried fruits and seeds in the
base of a clear pudding basin. Top with half
the rice mixture, then press down tightly and
smooth the top.

3 Spread the bean paste on top of the rice, and
top with the remaining rice mixture. Press down
and smooth the top.

4 Steam for 20 minutes and cool slightly, then
turn out onto a plate. Cut into small slices at
the table.

winter rice pudding with dried fruits

ingredients

SERVES 6–8

1 tbsp peanuts

1 tbsp pine kernels

1 tbsp lotus seeds

225 g/8 oz mixed dried fruits
(raisins, kumquats,
prunes, dates, etc.)

2 litres/3¹/₂ pints water

115 g/4 oz sugar

225 g/8 oz glutinous rice,
soaked in cold water for at
least 2 hours

method

1 Soak the peanuts, pine kernels and lotus seeds in a bowl of cold water for at least 1 hour. Soak the dried fruits as necessary. Chop all larger fruits into small pieces.

2 Bring the water to the boil in a saucepan, then add the sugar and stir until dissolved. Add the drained rice, nuts, lotus seeds and mixed dried fruits. Bring back to the boil. Cover and simmer over a very low heat for 1 hour, stirring frequently.

almond cookies

ingredients

MAKES ABOUT 50

675 g/1 lb 8 oz plain flour
$^1/_2$ tsp baking powder
$^1/_2$ tsp salt
100 g/3$^1/_2$ oz slivered almonds
225 g/8 oz vegetable fat, cut
    into tiny cubes
225 g/8 oz white sugar
1 egg, lightly beaten
1$^1/_2$ tsp almond extract
50 whole almonds,
    to decorate (optional)

method

1 Sift the flour, baking powder and salt together and set aside.

2 Pulverize the almond slivers in a food processor, then add the flour mixture and pulse until the nuts are well mixed with the flour.

3 Turn the flour and nut mixture into a large bowl, then add the vegetable fat and work into the flour until crumbly. Add the sugar, egg and almond extract and mix well until the dough is soft and pliable but still firm enough to be handled.

4 Divide the dough into small 2.5-cm/1-inch balls. Place the balls 5 cm/2 inches apart on an ungreased baking sheet and flatten them into circles with the back of a spoon. Press a whole almond into the centre of each, if liked.

5 Preheat the oven to 160°C/325°F/Gas Mark 3 and bake the cookies for 15–18 minutes, or until just beginning to brown, then remove and turn out onto a cooling rack.